THE MISSING LINK

ARTURO OROZCO

All rights reserved. The total or partial reproduction of this work is not allowed, nor its incorporation into a computer system, or its transmission in any form or by any means (electronic, mechanical, photocopying, recording, or otherwise) without the prior written permission of the copyright holder is a violation of these rights and may constitute a crime against intellectual property

The content of this work is the responsibility of the author and does not necessarily reflect the views of the publishing house. All texts and images were provided by the author, who is solely responsible for their rights.

References to the Bible correspond to the Reina Valera 1960 version.
The quotation is in parentheses, so it is paraphrased or a portion of the verse.

Published by Ibukku, LLC
www.ibukku.com
Cover Design: Ángel Flores Guerra Bistrain
Cover Photography: Arturo Orozco
Graphic Design: Diana Patricia González Juárez
Copyright © 2023 ARTURO OROZCO
ISBN Paperback: 978-1-68574-523-3
ISBN Hardcover: 978-1-68574-525-7
ISBN eBook: 978-1-68574-524-0

TABLE OF CONTENTS

Introduction 7

Section 1
Leaving the house 13
    Chapter 1
    The Two Sons 15
    Chapter 2
    Humanity's Dream 19
    Chapter 3
    Emancipation 23
    Chapter 4
    Beyond the Threshold 29
    Chapter 5
    The Distant Land 35
    Chapter 6
    The Unemployed Cherub 39
    Chapter 7
    The Missing Link 41
    Chapter 8
    The Man Who Wanted to Be an Animal 45
    Chapter 9
    The Day Laborers 51
    Chapter 10
    The Lost Coin 57

Section 2
Looking Back 63
    Chapter 11
    When Hunger Strikes 65
    Chapter 12
    Identity or ID Entity 71
    Chapter 13
    You Are Here 77
    Chapter 14
    Camel's Heart 81
    Chapter 15
    Closing One's Eyes 87

Chapter 16
The Theory Of R-evolution   93
Chapter 17
Imperfect Past Tense   99
Chapter 18
Intersections   101
Chapter 19
Heaven and Earth Kiss   105
Chapter 20
Standing in Front of the Estate   111

Section 3
The Return Home   115
Chapter 21
The Predestined Calf   117
Chapter 22
New Attire   121
Chapter 23
The Feast   127
Chapter 24
The Ring   131
Chapter 25
Footwear   135
Chapter 26
The Cherubim with a New Job   139
Chapter 27
New Residence   143
Chapter 28
Dressed for the Occasion   149
Chapter 29
God in a Box   155
Chapter 30
The Second Eve   159

To those who are tired of wandering
through life in search of a purpose.

To those who go through life
believing there is no purpose.

To those who go through life believing there's
nothing more at the end of the road.

Even to those who go through life hoping
someone finds the missing link...

I hope you find in this book
what you are looking for.

Introduction

A man wanted to build an estate. In his mind, there was an image of what he envisioned, every detail etched there. Everything seemed perfect.

He just needed to find the perfect location to build.

It had to be a place where the soil was fertile, where he could plant any kind of tree and see it bear fruit.

In his search, he found the perfect spot. Everything around it looked green. This was because nearby there was a river that branched into four streams, providing ample water for irrigation.

The ideal spot for his estate. He began construction. He aimed to create the best dwelling place for his children. He built a place that lacked nothing; his children wouldn't need to look elsewhere for anything to covet, for they would have everything.

He planted all kinds of trees so his children could eat their fruit.

And his children would become familiar with all types of trees. They would know the scents and the flavors. He wanted the best for them.

He had a wide variety of animals; some to help with the estate's chores, others for display and appreciation.

Upon completion, he put up a fence around it for protection and to mark the boundaries.

There was only one door, one entrance, which was on the eastern side of the estate.

Time passed and his children grew. They had everything they needed and were under their father's protection.

He taught them how to manage an estate, imparting the knowledge they needed at that point in time. He couldn't reveal all the secrets to them; it would be too much. Everything in its own time.

At that moment, it wasn't just about business and economics. He wanted to share with them how to be a good steward, a good person, a genuine human being, with integrity, ethics, and morality.

On one hand, he wished to share his heart, fostering a relationship that would last a lifetime, sharing all sorts of moments and experiences. More than anything, he wanted them to follow in his footsteps, to emulate him, to be like him.

Not to be him, but to be like him.

To represent him.

So, the father laid his heart bare for them to draw from.

On the other hand, the father shared his mind, his knowledge, his experience, his wisdom.

They needed that too, to excel, to succeed, to manage that place.

The father wouldn't let his children learn the hard way through falls or mistakes if he could prevent it.

As a parent, before teaching one's children how to earn their keep, one wants to teach them the basics of being a good, ethical person, manners, and morality. Only after they grasp these concepts do they get taught about work. There needs to be a balance.

Teach them to have ambition, but not greed.

To teach them it's good to desire, but not to covet.

They should aim to improve, but avoid taking shortcuts.

Here is the father, in one hand he holds his heart, they can come to him and feed on what he has to share with them.

Relationship, memories, foundation, connection.

In the other hand, he holds his brain, they can come and learn everything related to business, economics, wisdom, comfort.

Which hand would you choose?

What do you think you need more?

Which would take you further?

Which aligns more with your dreams?

Which of the two is more compatible with your plans?

I imagine the answers to these questions have a lot to do with the type of relationship we have with the father. Or with our perception of life or even of ourselves.

Here we have the younger son, looking at both hands and pondering what would benefit him most in life. He doesn't want to be like the father; he wants to be the father.

He desires independence but lacks the resources to have what the father has.

If he's going to disconnect from the father, he needs to take something that'll help him start his empire.

One day, the father will no longer be there, and everything around the younger son will be at his disposal. He will be the one making decisions about it.

He has to wait. One day he will receive his inheritance.

Wait? Wouldn't it be faster to live as if the father didn't exist and take what's mine?

To take his place and not have to answer to anyone for my actions?

And the son makes a decision, and asks the father for his share of the inheritance that belongs to him.

The younger son believes he is better than the father. He believes he can be a better administrator. In fact, he believes that he can have a better estate than the father's and a better way of managing it.

And he decides to take the father's brain, his knowledge, his wisdom, and leave that place to search for his own land where he can start anew and show his father that he is better.

The name of the younger son: Adam and Eve.

By now, I believe you've seen the contrast between the parable of the prodigal son and the story of the beginning of humanity in the Garden of Eden.

That the father (God), is in the garden sharing a relationship with his children.

And teaching them how to govern the earth and everything in it.

And that the hand with its heart is the tree of life, and the hand with its brain is the tree of knowledge.

When God created Adam, he equipped him with everything necessary to live on this earth.

When he placed him in the garden, he gave him missions to shape him and to give him a purpose, not just to exist, but a reason for doing so.

He implanted instincts in him that would help him seek development and improve every day.

In fact, man is told to satisfy these instincts...

Multiply, subdue, dominate, eat...

In addition to these instincts, he implanted something else, he breathed into his nostrils his own breath, which gave life to the human being. And besides life, that was what would connect him with God himself.

He made him in His image, similar to Him, so that he might represent Him, so that humans would seek ways to resemble Him, to be like Him.

Now we have, not just Adam, but what his name represents: humanity, looking at the trees and thinking about how the different fruits affect and benefit us.

We have humanity wishing to take only God's knowledge and depart, and act as if the father did not exist and not have to answer to anyone for what we do.

Not to be like the father, but to be the father himself, because we believe we could do a better job than him on this earth.

We can judge the prodigal son for what he did.

We can judge Adam for what he did.

But this isn't just their story, this is my story.

This could be your story.

This is the story of humanity searching for a purpose on this earth... Or maybe not.

Perhaps the story of humanity is just looking for an excuse not to have a purpose and just wander the world, living day by day...

SECTION 1
LEAVING THE HOUSE

Chapter 1
The Two Sons

He also said: A man had two sons;
Luke 15:11

So God created mankind in his own image, in the image of God he created them; male and female he created them.
Genesis 1:27

The Older Brother

He was a responsible, hardworking, dedicated person. The times he is mentioned in the story, he is found doing something, whether on the estate or in the field. This son took care of what belonged to the father. Although he was a son, he acted like a day laborer; he knew his position, but still felt he had to do more to please his father, do a bit more to earn the right to bring his friends over to his house for a party, even though he lived there and knew his rights. He still didn't believe he owned that property.

Even though he was told he could enjoy the benefits, he continued to believe it was too good to be true.

Being the firstborn, he knew that one day he would have to take charge of the estate.

But knowing that didn't make him understand that everything was his, as his father told him:

...You are always with me, and all that is mine is yours.
(Luke 15:31)

Perhaps the older brother didn't see his father as a father, but as a boss, the owner of the estate for whom he worked. And he, even knowing his position, acted as an employee, not as a son. Living in fear of disobeying, fearing that making a mistake could have serious consequences and result in punishment. Afraid that the owner of the estate had hidden cameras around the property and was always watching him, waiting for him to make a mistake to disinherit him. The older brother lived in fear of losing everything, even though everything belonged to him.

Are you surprised by the way I describe him? You'll be even more surprised to know that many people still live this way, seeing God as their God and not as a father. Living in fear of living because he sees everything. He hears everything. He knows everything.

I have talked to people who introspectively reflect on their lives every time they catch a cold because they believe they did something wrong to deserve that punishment. Once they fall ill, it's time to take stock of the past few weeks, thinking: I must have done something to deserve this cold.

There are people who have a relationship with God, but this relationship is based on fear, thinking that God might send punishments for disobedience, fearing of failing God or not doing his will because they believe that God could send a punishment.

I was one of them, always careful not to do or say anything wrong for fear of being disinherited. Always pushing myself a little harder not to react as I shouldn't, not to say what I shouldn't. Until I understood that God, before being God, is a father.

The older brother tried too hard, doing even the impossible to get his father's approval, to get a pat on the back, to get a reward.

The Younger Brother.

He appears as a more laid-back soul, brimming with curiosity, yearning to explore. Perhaps he wasn't wholly engrossed in the chores or tasks of the estate, rather, he spent his days venturing out, discovering new corners of the property, watching the laborers toil—perhaps pondering if he should learn their ways. He recognized he was a son, not a mere worker. He had the liberty to engage his father in potentially uncomfortable conversations, always inquisitive about the estate. He reveled in the place and its luxuries, partaking in whatever was served without a second thought.

He grasped his father's philosophy with perfect clarity: what's mine is yours. To the extent that the younger son was fully aware of his impending inheritance. In his heart, he believed he could lay claim to it whenever he chose. There was no need for him to earn his father's favor, nor live in fear of retribution.

Should he err, the younger brother knew his father was more than just a fleeting emotion; he was aware that their bond wasn't hinged on the whims of mood—it transcended temperament. Regardless of any upheavals, they'd persevere. The younger brother understood his place. Though it was in his nature to wander, he also knew that at day's end, there was always a home to return to.

I envision the father taking both sons to the supermarket. The younger son doesn't even bother asking for what he desires; he simply reaches out and takes it, certain of his standing. He knows his father won't deny him, confident that whatever he asks for, he will receive.

On the other hand, the elder son merely gazes longingly at his desires, debating whether he should muster the courage to request them from his father, his decision swaying based on his behavior that day.

Indeed, he might even slip his hand into his pocket, gauging if he has enough money to purchase what he craves, thinking he must earn his father's approval just to savor a treat. The father's grand design was for his sons to be reflections of him - that upon seeing them, one is reminded of the father, led to the father, and not just by the family name or shared physical features.

As I touched upon in the introduction, the father aims to cultivate character, ethics, and morality within his sons. To shape them in readiness to receive the legacy he has laid out for them. The genesis of this realization requires but a singular commitment: we must regard God as our father. He already perceives us as his children, yet we persist in our endeavors to earn His favor. Striving to please Him, trying to capture His gaze. Attempting to leave an impression.

The elder son might symbolize humanity's perception of God as depicted in the Old Testament: mankind toiling to secure God's favor by adhering to His commandments and precepts, hoping this would keep Him contented. Viewing Him as a deity perched on a distant throne, merely observing, waiting for mankind to falter so He might exact punishment. Humanity striving against odds to bridge the chasm between God and them, resorting to sacrifices in hopes of appeasing Him. All the while, aware of the promised inheritance but awaiting the right moment to claim it.

The younger son might symbolize humanity's perspective of God as portrayed in the New Testament: humanity recognizing that God desires to reveal Himself as a father, understanding that no sacrifice can purchase His favor, and knowing that we have direct access to that seemingly distant throne. We can converse with Him about any topic or situation, assured that He now perfectly grasps our sentiments.

Acknowledging that the father's blueprint is for us to mirror Him, to be His embodiment, and to strive to emulate His nature. Aware of the inheritance, and like the younger son, we can claim it today, should we so choose.

Chapter 2
Humanity's Dream

> *"But the younger of them said to his father, 'Father, give me the share of the estate that falls to me.' So he divided his wealth between them."*
> Luke 15:12

> *"For God knows that in the day you eat from it your eyes will be opened, and you will be like God, knowing good and evil."*
> Genesis 3:5

Imagine you have a dream, and within this dream, God stands before you and proclaims, "Ask of me whatever you wish!" What would you request? There are no boundaries; any desire that springs to mind, you can voice. What is it that you require most urgently at this very moment? What is that one thing which, if possessed, would grant you profound satisfaction? What is the sole ingredient that would infuse joy into your heart? What is the final puzzle piece that would bring the vast tapestry of your life to glorious completion?

Perhaps you never bothered to ponder upon such a question, for what are the odds of such an event transpiring? However, let me narrate the tale of one individual to whom this indeed occurred...

His name was Solomon. Freshly crowned, he began his reign over Israel.

He needed all the assistance he could muster to shoulder such a weighty responsibility. In his slumber, he dreams, and in this dream, God appears to him, offering to grant any wish he voices. God assures him that whatever he asks for, he shall receive. Absolutely anything.

Solomon's request? Wisdom (1 Kings 3:9).

He had the freedom to request anything his heart desired, and God even queried why he sought wisdom over a prolonged life. Once again, we see the father with open arms, offering himself without reservations.

And once more, humanity opts for what seems most beneficial in the immediate sense.

This brings to mind the Garden of Eden, where every conceivable need of humankind was met. At its heart stood two trees:

The Tree of the Knowledge of Good and Evil. Tasting its fruit would grant the eater the discernment between right and wrong, but also an awareness of pain, malice, fear, shame, and guilt – experiences and emotions they had been spared from.

The Tree of Life. Described in Revelation 22, this tree bore fruits that somehow extended the eater's life, and its leaves held healing properties. In Genesis 3, God even remarks that should man partake of the Tree of Life, he would live eternally.

It's as though Solomon stood before these two trees, forced to choose between them: one promising longevity, relationship, and communion with God, and the other offering knowledge to navigate life independently, without co-dependency.

As in the Garden of Eden, God laid bare both his heart and his intellect. Yet humanity, time and again, seems to prefer the intellect alone, believing it to be the key to attaining all desires.

Solomon knew of a higher existence. In the same chapter, in verse 6, he depicts the relationship between his father David and God. He speaks of David's heart being pure and upright before the Lord.

When God forged a covenant with David, once he had ascended the throne, David's sole desire was to build a dwelling for God, yearning to keep Him close. However, God informed David that it wasn't he, but his son Solomon, who would construct the house for God. Yet even after hearing this, David professed that his utmost wish was for God's name to be eternally exalted (2 Samuel 7:26).

Solomon realized that if he cultivated a heart-to-heart bond with God akin to David's, God would entrust him with His plans, and mold him, much like his father, to the extent that he would be heralded as a "Man after God's own heart" (Acts 13:22).

Yet such a relationship demands dependence. Solomon would have to relinquish his kingship, to allow himself to be governed by another. After all, he had a throne of his own to protect. So, Solomon reaches out, plucking fruit from the Tree of Knowledge. Bringing it close, he takes a bite.

He sought the mysteries of life before God's sacred secrets.

The wonders of creation, rather than the Creator Himself.

He craved merely God's intellect, not His heart.

Isn't this the dream of humanity?

To reign on our personal thrones, without answering to any higher power.

To determine for ourselves what's deemed right or wrong.

To live as if the Father isn't present.

Perhaps, if we suppress Him, He might just fade away.

To take what we believe is ours and depart from the estate, so that none can dictate our life's course.

Indeed, God mentioned to Solomon that one option available to him was to request a long life (v.11). Yet Solomon refrained, seeking only what he deemed essential to reign as king.

Later, in verse 14, God reveals the secret to a long life—a glimpse from the tree of life: that if Solomon binds his heart to God, as David, his father, once did, then he would enjoy many years.

Yes, he would attain success and wealth, but, in time, these treasures might sever him from God, altering his priorities.

Much like the prodigal son who took what he believed to be of utmost necessity, he would bask in riches and fame for a while, but would eventually lose connection with his father.

The tree proffered the knowledge to discern good from evil.

Yet, as Eve stood before it, she yearned for wisdom— wisdom, being the intricate blend of knowledge and experience.

Eve wished to bypass the journey, the time required to live and learn, in pursuit of this wisdom.

If there existed a means to possess omniscience— to foresee the outcome of a given situation based on our choices…

Without the mistakes,

Without the "I wish I had done that,"

Without the "I told you so,"

Without the "next time, I'll know better,"

Would it not be perfection?

Solomon believed so, and tasted of the tree.

Eva believed so, and tasted of the tree.

The prodigal son believed so, and tasted of the tree.

This brings me to ponder:

Could learning from another's mistakes be deemed wisdom?

Chapter 3
Emancipation

"Not many days later, GATHERING EVERYTHING, the younger son left and journeyed to a distant land..."
(Luke 15:13)

And the woman saw that the tree was good for food, and that it was pleasing to the eyes, and a tree to be desired to make one wise; she took of its fruit and ate, and gave also to her husband with her, and he ate.
(Genesis 3:6)

What might have been coursing through the younger son's mind when he asked his father for his share of the inheritance?

Did he pause, even for a brief moment, to consider how his father would feel upon hearing this?

Might he have chosen his words carefully, aiming for them to sound as reasonable as possible?

What could possibly have been troubling him within the estate, when everything he could ever desire was within arm's reach?

The father was the landowner, and according to the culture referenced in this parable, upon the father's passing, the inheritance would first go to the elder son. Only much later, upon the elder brother's demise, would the younger one benefit from the properties.

I can almost picture him, tallying up the years left before he could finally lay claim to this inheritance, with each sigh betraying the growing impatience within him.

Time, patience, process – these are terms to which we, at times, are reluctant to bind ourselves.

In the previous chapter, upon ascending to the throne, Solomon recognized his youthful inadequacy in leading the people. Yet, rather than wishing for more years of life, time to undergo the process of learning and experiencing, he chose to sidestep this natural evolution, yearning instead for wisdom. Similarly, in the Garden of Eden, Eve believed that having omniscient knowledge would elevate her to godhood.

All three got what they desired. But the ensuing challenge was discerning how to wield such newfound gifts. Solomon sought comprehension of the universe, Eve craved the fruit in her quest for divine equivalence, and the younger son yearned for wealth and independence.

Observing this pattern, it's evident that all three sought self-definition, eschewing the shadows or Images of others; they yearned for independence.

Delving into the psyche of the prodigal son provides a panoramic insight into the human condition.

Our "Adam" represents our moral side, capable of forging a connection with the Divine. He embodies the essence of our relationship with God, mirroring His image. Upon creation, Adam could freely roam the garden, unburdened by inhibition, devoid of secrets. The bond between them was pure, marked by harmonious connection. Adam's heart echoed the rhythm of God's own beat.

On the other hand, our "Eve" symbolizes our perceptive core: our senses, rationale, and sensibilities. It was she who wandered the garden, driven by curiosity – to see, smell, touch, taste, and grasp the realm around her. Grounded in reality, she served as our tether to tangible existence.

While Adam was present, there was a safeguard against severing that divine link; a guiding purpose was evident. Adam, acquainted with God, was attuned to His desires. But then, one fateful day, Adam fell into a deep slumber, allowing Eve her own agency. (Genesis 2:21)

She began to explore the garden, yearning for deeper fulfillment, and in her wanderings, she envisioned becoming more – perhaps even another version of herself. The idea of self-definition became tantalizing, the lure of ascending to godhood irresistible.

Though expressly forbidden, Eve found herself inexorably drawn to the tree, captivated and coveting its fruit. One can't help but speculate that had Adam been at her side, he might have dissuaded her from temptation; for her protection was his duty.

I suspect Eve intentionally distanced herself from Adam, drawn by the allure of the forbidden tree. She believed that by partaking of its fruit, she'd possess the wisdom to discern good from evil independently.

And so, she tasted the fruit, as if claiming an early inheritance.

Not content with her solo act of defiance, she beckoned Adam to join her, to align with her newfound perspective. Their eyes were suddenly opened, but not in the way they might have anticipated.

The innocence and freedom they once enjoyed, wandering the garden unashamed, transformed into deep-seated shame. Adam's intimate communion with God now mutated into fear, prompting them to hide. A survival instinct, previously unnecessary in Eden's paradise, now took hold.

This newfound drive to rival God transformed into a game of hide and seek: a challenge to see if they could evade the omnipotent.

Their guilt bred defensive mechanisms, attempts to rationalize their actions. Adam lost dominion; everything that God had declared good was now tainted in their perception. Control slipped from his grasp.

Eve no longer desired definition through another's lens. She refused to merely reflect another's image...

The younger son, perhaps unwittingly, conveys a grim message when he requests his share of the inheritance. In essence, he wishes for his father's death, for that would be the traditional path to inheritance. In making this request, he seems to be declaring his yearning for his father's absence, to escape the father's overarching shadow, to be free of his influence. The younger son wishes to sever this bond, to let the Adamic side of him rest, to sever the umbilical cord connecting him to his past and lineage.

We see the younger son yearning to be the patriarch of his narrative.

We find Adam and Eve skulking in the shadows, avoiding accountability for their choices.

This brings to mind Solomon. With his unparalleled wisdom, did he truly know how to wield it? As the tale of Solomon unfolds, we see that, over time, he drifts away from God. His vulnerability lay in his multitude of wives, particularly those foreign to his faith. These women, devoted to their own pantheons, seemed to have a pull on Solomon that was even stronger than his bond with God. He began endorsing their beliefs, constructing shrines and idols for their deities.

Rather than emulating the image of God, Solomon started to craft his own deities. He turned from being a creation of God to a creator of gods.

Romans chapter 1 mirrors this narrative. It speaks of humanity's evolution in recognizing the divine. While God manifested Himself in myriad ways, and even though humans were aware of His existence, they chose not to acknowledge Him as such. Claiming wisdom, they became fools, their reasoning clouded. Instead of venerating God, they chose to mold their own deities in their likeness, seeking to replace Him.

What intrigues me is that the very chapter also mentions that despite their decisions, God allowed them their autonomy.

If we seek inheritance, like the prodigal son, He grants it to us.

If we yearn for the wisdom of the world, He bestows it upon us.

If we wish to taste the fruit of knowledge to define our own selves, He permits it.

We possess free will, an inalienable right that no one can strip away.

But are we truly equipped to handle all that comes with such choices?

Chapter 4
Beyond the Threshold

> *NOT MANY DAYS LATER, the younger son gathered all he had and set out to distant lands.*
> (Luke 15:13)
>
> *And he said, "I heard the sound of you in the garden, and I was afraid, because I was naked, and I hid myself."*
> (Genesis 3:10)

The younger son had made his choice; he would depart from home. The estate had but one gate, facing the east. An intriguing aspect of the parable is the speed with which the younger son made his exit; it wasn't many days after his request. With everything he possessed in his hands, it seemed he had no need to delay or strategize.

And so, he began his journey eastward. Casting a last lingering look at the estate, he realized there was no turning back. Crossing the threshold, a few steps later, the gate shut behind him.

While pondering over humanity's beginnings from the book of Genesis, I noticed a recurring motif. When Adam and Eve were expelled from Eden, it seems there was but one entrance, situated to the east. That very gateway had a cherubim set to guard the path leading back.

They ventured eastward, and it was understood that should they ever wish to return, they would need to retrace their steps and plead their case before God.

As time passed, one of their own, Cain, erred grievously, taking the life of his brother. When God confronted him on his actions, Cain's response was to depart from that place, venturing further east, distancing himself even more from Eden.

They began to multiply, and with each successive generation, it seemed they discovered novel ways to indulge their desires. A point was reached where wickedness became so rampant that God gazed upon humanity and chose to unleash the flood, intending to start anew.

Some time after the deluge, a vast congregation of souls sought purpose, yearning for something to define them. Curiously, after what seemed an eternity, they decided to change their trajectory. Instead of continuing eastward, Genesis 11 notes they emerged from the east.

They reached a vast plain, spacious enough for all, and there they settled. In this place, an idea was birthed: to erect a city crowned with a tower soaring to the heavens. Their ambition was to craft, by their own hands, a conduit to the celestial realms, and they would christen it "Babel", meaning "God's Gate".

They envisioned constructing something that even God would recognize as a gateway to heaven, to carve out their unique destiny, and be hailed as the generation that unveiled heaven's entrance. Those who realized they needed not be mere reflections of others to fulfill mankind's purpose.

As they embarked on this grand endeavor, it was with God in mind, contemplating the potential of a portal through which one might ascend to heaven and commune with the Divine. Hence, the name they bestowed upon it.

As they stood on that plain, with God watching over them from above, all they needed to do was lift their eyes heavenward, present their case, and God would unveil a doorway to reconnect.

But such an act would render them vulnerable, reliant. To construct their own gateway to the heavens meant risking exposure to perceived weakness; it would portray them as unsure, as adrift, as if in dire need of guidance.

When God fashioned Adam and Eve, He imparted directives, bequeathing a purpose. He instructed them to multiply, to fill the earth, to scatter across its vast expanses. Similarly, post-deluge, as they emerged from the ark, the edict remained unchanged: to disperse and populate the world.

Yet, they harbored desires to remain unified, eschewing the idea of venturing and exploring disparate lands individually.

And here they stood, aspiring to build a tower scaling the heavens. In a bid for renown, they sought to mirror the inception of humanity, echoing the moment when God sculpted man from clay, a likeness of His form on earth.

In turn, they now harnessed the clay to mold bricks, endeavoring to craft a monument symbolizing their collective spirit. A structure so imposing that any wandering soul merely had to glimpse its towering silhouette to discern the way back to the fold. They yearned to carve out a novel purpose autonomously.

They refused to stand as mere reflections of another. Their ambition was to emerge as the paramount figures in their narratives.

This wasn't their terminal endeavor. In time, they embarked on sculpting their own pantheon. Deities of fertility, of harvest, and of war were conceived. These self-made gods were endowed with purpose and persona. Eventually, these divinities were envisaged as servile to man's desires.

From clay, metal, and timber, whatever lay before them was employed to forge guardians, entities empowered to bestow upon them their every want and need.

And in time, they would devise rituals, believing that such ceremonies would compel their gods into action. Sacrifices would be crafted, thinking these offerings would curry favor and fulfill their myriad requests.

They now fashioned gods, with humanity taking center stage, or so they believed.

> *"For although they knew God, they neither glorified him as God nor gave thanks to him, but their thinking became futile and their foolish hearts were darkened."*
> Romans 1:21

What then was the essence of their emancipation? Why did the younger son yearn to depart from his home? He sought self-definition, desiring autonomy irrespective of the absence of a clear plan or purpose. The idea of reliance on another's decisions was stifling. He aimed to be the hero of his own narrative, even if he was unsure of how to navigate the plot.

To embody the reflection of another mandates the fulfillment of a set purpose. It necessitates directives, it calls for submission. If we aren't molded in anyone else's image, we aren't bound by their directives, nor obligated to follow another's purpose. We claim dominion over our lives, uninhibited by external mandates.

Even if our life journey spans merely from birth to growth, procreation, and eventual demise – it remains our sovereign choice. Even if we squander the grandest of destinies, the prerogative is ours. We are averse to letting others chart our course.

Initially, humanity had a purpose.

The younger son, too, was destined for a purpose.

We each have a purpose in this life. Yet, much like Solomon, to fulfill it, we must step down from our self-imposed thrones and yield to the divine, allowing Him to guide our decisions and realize our purpose. We must circle back to that gateway, presenting our case before God. We must surrender, becoming a reflection of something beyond ourselves. What a momentous decision lies ahead.

Even if we've passed through the door, and it has closed behind us, it's not the end. The direction we choose, where our inner compass points, is guided by something called free will – a gift that God respects, allowing us our autonomy.

What will be our next step?

What will be our next choice?

Chapter 5
The Distant Land

> *"...The younger son traveled to a distant province, and there he squandered his wealth in wild living."*
> (Luke 15:13)

> *"So He drove the man out, and at the east of the Garden of Eden, He stationed cherubim with a flaming, whirling sword to guard the way to the tree of life."*
> Genesis 3:24

When Adam and Eve were instructed not to eat from the tree of knowledge, they were told that consumption would bring death. It seems that when God spoke of death, He referred more to a spiritual state than a physical one: a disconnection. It's as if something inside Adam would cease to function, something would dim, a vital essence would be lost. This becomes evident as, after their transgression, they continued to live, albeit in a radically changed manner. Moreover, one of the consequences of tasting that forbidden fruit was the denial of access to another fruit - the tree of life, which granted prolonged existence and health.

Within the Garden, Adam had been vested with authority. God commanded him to rule over the animals, to exercise dominion over them. As long as Adam remained in communion with God, he was empowered with such authority.

To explain this, I found the story of another biblical character who experienced the same thing: Nebuchadnezzar. He was the king of Babylon.

God allowed him to conquer and rule this empire so that he could fulfill God's plans. But one day, Nebuchadnezzar began to see things differently. He began to believe that everything he did and owned was due to his own achievement and effort.

One day, he had a dream, and in that dream, it showed him what happens when you want to break free from God and live without being ruled by anyone.

When you want to eat the fruit of knowledge to take control of your affairs and do things your way.

When you covet wisdom and only want knowledge, the wisdom of the Father, to govern your life without being the reflection or shadow of someone else.

In the Book of Daniel, Chapter 4, Nebuchadnezzar's dream is recounted.

In this dream, he saw a large tree that reached the sky, and this tree could be seen from all the ends of the earth. It bore abundant fruit, the beasts of the field rested under its shade, and everyone was sustained by this tree.

As long as Nebuchadnezzar allowed himself to be ruled by God, the tree would remain this way.

But his intentions began to change because, having gained all that power and authority, it was time to break free from God and withdraw from the relationship with the part of the inheritance that belonged to him.

In that same dream, he was shown what happens when you do that. Nebuchadnezzar saw someone descending from the heavens in his dream, giving the order for the tree to be cut down.

Once the tree is cut down, there is no more fruit to give; the leaves dry up, and what struck me most is that it mentions the beasts that were resting in the shade of the tree depart from there. They are awakened, the animal side is awakened, instincts come alive and take over the heart. A man's heart is replaced with a beast's heart.

> *'Let his mind be changed from that of a man*
> *and let a beast's mind be given to him...'*
> (Daniel 4:16)

Just like Nebuchadnezzar, Adam wanted to be his own king, make his own decisions, be like God. So he ate from the tree of knowledge, and in doing so, automatically renounced the tree of life and its benefits.

Now he would know good and evil, hunger, sickness, death, fatigue, nakedness, shame... but he would be his own king, and this, his new kingdom.

Nebuchadnezzar made the same decision. God warned him in that dream that if he wanted to be his own king, if he wanted to compare himself to God, then He would give him his kingdom, a kingdom where God would step aside until Nebuchadnezzar decided to seek Him and recognize that God is the only king.

> *'So that the living may know that the Most High*
> *is sovereign over all kingdoms on earth...'*
> (Daniel 4:17)

What Nebuchadnezzar did not know was that the gigantic tree connecting him to heaven was the only thing keeping the beasts at rest.

Nebuchadnezzar didn't know that the moment these awoke, his perception would change, his entire life would take a drastic turn. But like any human being, he had to go through something like this to understand and perhaps learn a great lesson.

That's what God was referring to when He mentioned they would die if they chose to taste that tree.

The tree that connected heaven and earth, the tree that was the link between God and men, the tree that nourished the relationship between them, would be cut down.

And they might be physically in the same place, but spiritually, man would have traveled to a distant land.

The younger son is on his way to a distant land, to the unknown. Without his father to warn him of the risks or dangers he might encounter out there. But that's what the son wanted, to be his own image, to make a name for himself, to rely on his decisions.

His own will takes the crown of the kingdom, walks to the throne, sits on it.

It reclines and takes a look at its new kingdom.

The first order it gives is... Keep walking.

The father gave him what he wanted, the part of the inheritance that was his due.

He can't stop him; it's the son's decision.

We have made a decision, to emancipate ourselves, but every decision has consequences.

But we don't want anyone to tell us what might happen out there, in the distant land.

The father stretched out his hands; in one was his connection, his heart; in the other his knowledge, his brain, and we chose to take the brain and withdraw.

What seemed to be the dream of humanity could end up being a nightmare.

Chapter 6
The Unemployed Cherub
(Reflection)

Adam and Eve are being covered in animal skins.
Something had to be sacrificed to provide clothing.
An animal had to pay for what they had done.
They exchanged a connection with God for the tree of knowledge.
Perception overpowered intuition.
A craving overcame their integrity.
No, not a craving, a whim.
Now they are walking towards the exit, the only door to the garden.
This door faces the east.
All their comforts are history; they now
must learn to earn their bread.
They have to figure out how to protect themselves. Hopefully,
all the knowledge in their heads will help them survive.
Let's hope they find ways to thrive.
As they walk out, they gaze upon the trees they once enjoyed.
Now they will encounter thorns, weeds, and shrubs.
To know which they can eat and which
not, they'll have to take risks.
They cross the door, they're outside.
Everything around them is new.
And they keep walking.
Instructions are given to a cherub: guard the door.
He's handed a sword to deter anyone who might want to enter.
Humans are persistent, but in the state they're
in, they can't return to the garden.

They can't taste the tree of life.
The cherub will need that sword to stop them.
The cherub stands at the door, on guard.
He will defend the path to the tree of life at all costs.
It's his job. It's his mission.

Time goes by, and humans multiply.
And the more they grow, they move further east.
Further away from the garden.
Further away from the door.
A moment comes when the cherub is confused.
He expected humans to seek the tree of life.
To want to return, to want to make their case before God,
Negotiate with God.
But they are not interested.
They found new ways to distract themselves.

New ways to keep themselves busy.
New ways to suppress those needs.
New ways to replace them.
Time passes, and humans multiply,
equal to their malice.
And they keep distancing.
A moment comes when the cherub is worried.
No one has approached since the day Adam
and Eve walked out that door.
No one has approached out of curiosity.
The flaming sword in his hand is dimming.
It seems he doesn't need it, after all.

Time goes by, and humans multiply.
And they keep moving, further and further away.
The cherub has become a statue.
Sitting on a stone, looking at the ground.
He was given a task, and he was ready.
But there was no one who wanted to return.
There was no one looking back.
And time keeps passing...

Chapter 7
The Missing Link

> *"And he went and joined himself to a citizen of that country; and he sent him into his fields to feed swine."*
> Luke 15:16

> *"And unto Adam also and to his wife did the LORD God make coats of skins, and clothed them."*
> Genesis 3:21

The younger son left his father's estate, made his decision, believing that with the portion of inheritance he had received, he could travel the world and revel in his emancipation, thinking that what he had would never run out.

Then came the day he opened his wallet and realized that his understanding of wealth and management was far from his new reality. His fun had run out; it was time to make new decisions. It seemed that the wealth he thought he had gave him his identity. Once this ran out, his self-perception began to change. He no longer saw himself as a son; he no longer viewed himself as a member of a family he could return to and try to start over. He needed a new self-concept, a new perception of himself, a new identity.

When he was near his father, he knew who he was; he was the younger son.

Once separated from him, he felt the need for someone else to convince him of who he truly was.

He approached the owner of another estate, seeking an identity.

Looking to belong.

Searching for adaptation.

The owner of this other estate didn't need a son; he needed an employee.

This person wasn't going to waste the opportunity to recruit someone to feed the pigs. The owner of the other estate wasn't going to persuade the younger son to return home to his father as long as he needed workers.

The young man was confused, not knowing who he was, easily manipulated.

He was desperate, hungry, willing to eat anything, accept any salary, and grasp at the first opportunity given to him.

The risk he took was that if he adopted another identity that wasn't his own, he would lose his purpose, his sense of existence, what he was made for.

He would fall into a routine: be born, grow up, reproduce, die.

Wake up in the mornings, go out to feed the pigs, fulfill his schedule, return to his room, sleep, and expect the same the next day.

What for? For how much longer? What's the purpose of all this?

For a long time, people have sought evidence to prove that we descend from monkeys. That we are nothing more than animals that evolved, that we are the product of an explosion that occurred millions of years ago.

That there's nothing after death.

That we forget that someone is waiting for us at the other estate.

That we aren't sons, but merely day laborers born to feed animals.

Though, I believe this can only be taken as an excuse to behave like animals.

To justify our actions with the phrase: "I'm only human!"

And we keep desperately digging in different parts of the earth for that evidence, that ticket that will grant us permission to react and act as we please, in the end, we're just animals.

We won't have to answer to anyone for our behavior.

Until today, it's only a theory, and even though we might want to be convinced that it's a fact, we continue living as day laborers, adapting to a new identity.

We're told that our job is to feed animals.

To clothe ourselves with animal skins or with a stamp that we descend from monkeys to justify ourselves. To appear as victims who can't control their instincts, wearing masks so people can't see our true intentions. Forgetting about character and confusing it with temperament to say: "That's just the way I am!"

Do you remember chapter five?

When Nebuchadnezzar wanted to emancipate, the tree connecting him to heaven was cut down. What kept the beasts dormant was removed, and they awoke.

And they took control to such an extent that it's mentioned even his heart was changed to that of a beast.

An animal that only seeks satisfaction, that only wants to obtain what it desires, regardless of whether it's taken from someone else.

Regardless of whether someone else gets hurt.

When Adam and Eve left paradise, before they departed, they were given clothing. Made from animal skins. What had been created in the image of God now walked outside of paradise covered in animal hide. After having lived naked in paradise, they had to cover their nudity and the cold; they couldn't be vulnerable.

Before, animal skins were used to protect against the cold; now we use human "skin" to shield or sometimes hide the coldness of our hearts.

To not expose our feelings and appear weak, to seem like easy prey.

They couldn't show their weakness; they couldn't be transparent.

They were leaving paradise to enter the jungle. Where they had to protect themselves, had to intimidate, had to pretend; now it was about eat or be eaten.

Years have passed, and the story continues, now that animal disguise has become our new identity. It's not just the skin anymore; like Nebuchadnezzar, the heart has been transformed, and the only thing that keeps us going is to keep feeding the animal so that it feeds us back.

To the point of finding our identity in that animal.

And we don't just settle for that, on the contrary, we'd feel thrilled if this theory became fact. Because that would justify humanity.

It would justify us to ourselves.

And it would be a pass to not have to answer to anyone for what we do.

The saddest part of this is, if we continue like this, years from now, there will be animals digging up the earth, looking for a homo sapiens skull to prove that we were once human.

That there indeed was someone waiting for us at the other estate.

Chapter 8
The Man Who Wanted to Be an Animal

> *"And he would gladly have filled his belly with the husks that the swine ate: and no man gave unto him."*
> Luke 15:16

> *"Thorns also and thistles shall it bring forth to thee; and thou shalt eat the herb of the field."*
> Genesis 3:18

The younger son is working on a different estate, where they made him believe he's just a laborer, that he has to work feeding the pigs.

However, it seems the wage or the food he was receiving was not enough; it wasn't the same sustenance he used to get at home.

So, he eyed the pig's food and wanted to eat from it.

What does it mean to eat animal feed?

When God created the animals, He used His word and commanded them into existence.

He said let the earth produce living creatures, and they came to be (Genesis 1:24).

But when He created man, He personally shaped him from the dust of the ground, and when He finished molding him, He breathed into his nostrils the breath of life.

He breathed into him the spirit of life.

A part of God remained within Adam.

And that spirit was the connection between God and Adam.

That spirit, once we depart from this world, returns to God.

That spirit transcends the limitations of the body.

That spirit seeks eternity.

The point of all this is that animals lack a spirit, once they die, it's over.

As a human being, one has to cross over and return to

God. This is just the beginning.

But we wish it wasn't like that; we would want to convince ourselves that there's nothing after death.

We would hope that when we die, there wouldn't be anything beyond, so we wouldn't have to deal with the consequences of what we did on this earth.

We want to eat animal food, be like them, who don't have to worry about accounting for their actions.

We want to believe that we are just something that arose from an explosion and that there's no purpose in being in this world.

But it's not like that; the reality is different.

How easy it would be for us to know that there's truly nothing after death.

That we can do whatever we want without worrying about the consequences.

If it were that easy, suicide would be the solution to all our problems.

Just say goodbye and disappear forever.

But no matter how low we fall, no matter how stressful life might be, no matter how painful facing consequences could be, we're still here.

We don't want to cross to the other side; we don't want to face what lies beyond death.

When Cain, the son of Adam and Eve, killed his brother Abel, he was dressed in animal skins; in fact, he was acting like an animal, impulsively, without measuring the consequences.

The only thing that concerned him when God confronted him for what he had done was that he didn't want to die.

"Behold, you have driven me out this day from the face of the ground; and from Your face I will be hidden, and I will be a vagrant and a wanderer on the earth, and whoever finds me will kill me."

(Genesis 4:14).

He said to God: Yes, I will leave this land, far from you; yes, I will be hiding from your presence, (as if he could pretend that God does not exist).

Yes, I will go to another distant land, where I'll be a stranger, where nobody knows me, (it seems another version of the prodigal son parable), but I don't want to die; I don't want to leave this world.

Even if we wish to live eating animal food, and keep pretending that one day we'll vanish into nothingness, we're still here.

Something within us doesn't want to face death, because that something, and I'm referring to our spirit, seeks eternity.

Deep down, we know that everything doesn't end when we die.

That spirit within us is the real missing link.

What if, instead of continuing to dig the earth to prove that we are just animals that evolved to keep justifying that we only want to eat animal food to evade reality, we better dig within ourselves.

And look within us to find the missing link that shows us we are not animals, that we transcend after death. It doesn't all end in a grave.

Once we dig into our heart and find that evidence, then we will understand what a true human being is. Knowing that we are eternal within us will give us a new perspective, a new identity, a purpose to exist and be the best version of ourselves, knowing that one day we will reconnect with the Father.

When Adam and Eve were in paradise, they were naked before God and were not ashamed, because that connection with God changes priorities.

Once they disconnected from God, the physical became a priority for them, and they had to cover themselves because they began to feel shame.

We want to hide behind animal skins, but we are much more than that. Now we have Adam and Eve outside of paradise. When they were connected to God, they could eat from the fruit of the trees in the garden.

Once they left, they were destined to eat grass from the field, which is what the animals ate. "To every beast of the earth, to every bird of the sky, and to everything that creeps on the earth, in which there is life, every green plant will be for food." And it was so (Genesis 1:30). Imagine the scene: Adam, created in the image of God, with an animal skin tunic, in the field, bent over, pulling up herbs to eat.

Imagine the scene: the younger son inside the pigpen, stained with the mud where the pigs live. Hungry, to the point of stretching out his hand, battling in his mind with what remains of his humanity, wanting to grab a piece of the food the pigs are enjoying to quench his hunger.

King Nebuchadnezzar's dream came true. Since he wanted to be his own king, God stepped aside, and he was allowed to emancipate himself. His perception changed; his heart was transformed into the heart of a beast. He left the palace and roamed the fields, among the oxen, eating grass from the ground (Daniel 4:33).

We all reach this situation of our own accord; it's our decision.

All of this will change when we start to change our diet and begin to consume human food. God himself told Nebuchadnezzar, you will stop eating like an animal, until you recognize that there is a God, that there's a spiritual world, and therefore, a spirit exists.

Chapter 9
The Day Laborers

> *... treat me as one of your laborers.*
> (Luke 15:19)

> *... And they woke him up, saying, "Master, do you not care that we are perishing?"*
> (Mark 4:38)

The Storm

Once, while Jesus was teaching in a place, dusk began to fall. Jesus had plans for the next day, people to free, lives to change.

He told his disciples to cross to the other side of the Sea of Galilee.

They climbed into the boat, set off, and Jesus fell asleep.

On their way to the other side, a storm broke out. From the way it's described, it seemed like something they were not used to.

The boat began to be violently tossed about, and the disciples started to fear for their lives. It looked like the very boat they were traveling in would be torn apart. Yet Jesus remained asleep.

They had forgotten two very crucial things.

First, before climbing into the boat, Jesus shared the plan: "Let's go to the other side."

Jesus had given them a purpose for boarding the boat.

The reason they were sailing was because there was a destination.

Second, more than half of those disciples had been fishermen before Jesus called them. They had been in such situations before. They knew how to react, they knew what to do to get out of such a predicament; they had experience.

But one thing is true, no matter how good you are at navigating, no matter how prepared you are for the storms along the way, no matter how ready you are to respond to circumstances, we will always need help.

There will come a time, a situation, that makes us look upwards, that makes us question ourselves, that lets us know how vulnerable we can be.

A situation that invites us to awaken Jesus.

Where was God?

Have you ever heard this question?

Have you ever asked yourself this?

Typically, we ask this question when we are in a situation that is, or has gone, out of control. Sometimes it's challenging to answer this question for ourselves for the simple reason that we only ask it after we've tried every possible method, and the last resort is to look above, seeking someone to blame.

We don't pose this question seeking a solution; we just want a target where we can project our frustration, and sometimes, our anger.

If we asked ourselves this question every day, even when everything is going as we wish, it would be easier to find the answer to that very question in our lowest moments, because He is always in the same place.

Even the disciples in the boat, when everything was going according to the plan, Jesus fell asleep and they didn't mind. They kept talking, socializing, sailing.

When the storm broke out and they saw they couldn't control the situation, even thinking they might perish, believing it was the end of the road, that's when they remembered that Jesus was in the same boat with them.

They rushed to wake him, and the first thing they asked was: "Do you not care that we are perishing?" (Mark 4:38)

What are you doing during my storm?

Don't you care about what I'm going through?

Shouldn't you, being God, take control?

Is this why you had me board this boat?

The Day Laborers

When the younger son was still on his father's estate, every day he would watch the laborers, his father's employees. They worked on the estate, had a task, a schedule, a responsibility, and a payday.

Perhaps many of these laborers spent so much time out in the fields or were so engrossed in their duties that they didn't notice when the estate owner strolled by them, or checked on how tasks were progressing throughout the estate.

Perhaps many of the laborers didn't even know the owner.

They only worked there because someone else brought them to that place or they heard stories of the estate owner through people who had seen him or spoken to him.

Perhaps, the only time they were convinced of the owner's existence was on payday, when they received something for the work they were doing, for the tasks they were carrying out.

Maybe when the paycheck they expected was a bit delayed or didn't arrive at the exact moment they were waiting for, they began to say:

"What? Is no one in charge of this estate?

What is the owner of this place doing?

Doesn't he know I need my pay to continue with my life?

Why doesn't he act as he should?

Where is the owner of this place when I'm hungry?"

The Boat

Our life is like the boat the disciples were in with Jesus. Just like them, we received the invitation to board, and we did, and now we are here.

Just as they were given a purpose—to cross to the other side—for us, it might be to get through this day, to get through a journey, to overcome a problem, to travel from point A to point B.

When we embarked on this journey, on this voyage, we did so with a connection to God.

With a part of Him that pushes us to seek Him, to call upon Him.

But we believe the journey would be more comfortable if Jesus fell asleep, if God kept His distance, if instead of being children, we were laborers who just worked on this estate.

We believe it would be more comfortable to think that He isn't there, and that we can act as we wish, that we can be ourselves.

Instead of a God, we'd like to have a genie in a lamp, and that we'd only have to talk to him when we're in a situation that's getting out of control.

We'd want to have a sleeping Jesus in the boat, only waking Him up to calm the storms and bring peace back to our day, and then let Him return to sleep.

We'd want an employer there every weekend to give us the paycheck for what we did during that time.

And not have to deal with the responsibilities of being a son or daughter.

We don't want a relationship that commits us, a relationship where we have to give too much, to the point of risking who we are. Having to stop being who I am to become something or someone else.

We'd wish for this genie to come out of the lamp and say: "Make a wish, whatever you want."

I think I know what we'd ask for:

"Make me like one of your laborers!"

Chapter 10
The Lost Coin

"I am no longer worthy to be called your son;"
(Luke 15:19)

"Or what woman having ten drachmas, if she loses one drachma, does not light a lamp, sweep the house, and search diligently until she finds it?"
Luke 15:8

When one commits to marriage, there is a custom or tradition known as the "arras" or tokens.

This represents a deposit or a pledge that the person offering them is going to protect and, above all, provide for the other person.

They are going to take care of the other person.

In other cultures, these tokens are interpreted as the wedding ring.

A representation of fidelity, and the notion that the two are now one.

In a way, they belong to each other.

But what happens if this wedding ring is lost? What if this symbol is neglected?

This doesn't mean that the couple is automatically separated, or that what truly binds them is this ring, but it's a symbol.

This which is worn on the hand represents that commitment.

When Jesus told the parable of the lost coin, this is what he was referring to.

The point of the parable was to put the listeners in the shoes of the woman who had lost her ring or her tokens, so that those hearing the parable could identify with the woman's desperation.

And that's what we'll do...

When we come into this world, we arrive with that connection, with that integrity, open to believing in a supreme being who created us and watches over us.

This connection is in the spirit.

And Ecclesiastes 12:7 mentions that once we depart from this world, the spirit returns to God who gave it to us, who breathed that breath, that part of Him, into us.

That spirit within us is what makes us His, what makes us belong to Him, it's like that wedding ring placed on us to symbolize that we are one with Him.

That spirit is what motivates us to seek Him, to believe in Him, to believe that there's something much larger than ourselves.

That there is a spiritual kingdom, that we possess more than just what we can see, hear, or touch.

This spirit's purpose is to connect with God Himself.

Ephesians 1:13-14 states that once we believe in Him, we were sealed with the promised Holy Spirit, which is the guarantee of our inheritance until we become His possession.

2 Corinthians 1:22 mentions that God has sealed us, and has given us the pledge of the Spirit in our hearts.

2 Corinthians 5:4-5 mentions that even though we are in this fleshly body, we yearn for the mortal to be absorbed by the eternal, as if something within us is conscious of eternity even though this body has an expiration date.

It also mentions that the one who designed us this way is God, who gave us the pledge of the Spirit.

We were designed to seek Him, to yearn for, to desire Him, so why don't we?

In the parable of the prodigal son, he decides to leave the estate, he chooses to emancipate himself, he has free will to chart his own course.

In the parable of the lost coin, the woman loses the coin.

Accident?

Neglect?

Distraction?

She knows she lost it, knows she must find it at all costs.

She knows that if the person who gave her that coin finds out she lost it, she will have to provide a very good explanation. The woman is desperate. Anxious.

She will meet her husband at any moment.

He is going to walk through the door at any moment.

They will face each other, and he will notice a coin is missing.

The husband will walk through the door and see her without the ring on her finger.

We've journeyed through this world, we've been careless, we've been distracted, and we've lost that ring that symbolizes that we belong to Him.

We are aware that at any moment we will stand before the one who gave us that ring. We will need to have the best explanation to get out of such a situation.

We'll have to present our best case to be excused from something like that.

We have three options:

The first, to resign ourselves and wait to see how this ends.

The second, to find the best explanation.

The third, to search for that ring, to search for that coin, and find it.

This coin meant so much to the woman in the parable, so much so that when she found it, she called her friends and neighbors and told them they should rejoice with her because she found what she had lost.

Losing something like that should show our desperation, and that desperation should push us to move everything within our being to find that coin.

To search even in the darkest corners of our hearts to find that piece so indispensable to our life.

To search for that missing link that shows us we are much more than just animals.

To seek that lost link that connects us with someone much greater than ourselves.

That missing link that leads us to the being to whom we belong.

In the parable of the lost coin, the woman moved everything inside her house.

She moved everything inside her house to make spaces where there weren't any, just to find it.

If you believe your heart is too dark to do something like this at this point in your life, that's what the lamp is for, to illuminate those corners and search there.

If you believe your heart is too dirty to find even a glimpse of God there, that's what the broom is for, to start cleaning and removing what might be obscuring it.

She was desperate.

How desperate are you?

The next section of this book will help us search for that valuable piece that has gone astray.

So I invite you to take your lamp and your broom.

We have to find it.

SECTION 2
LOOKING BACK

Chapter 11
When Hunger Strikes

"And when he had spent everything, a severe famine arose in that country, and he began to be in need."
Luke 15:14

"And inasmuch as they commanded to leave the stump of the tree roots, your kingdom will be assured to you, after you recognize that Heaven rules."
Daniel 4:26

The prodigal son has had his fill of fun, he has spent on whatever he wanted, there were no limits for him. Whatever he wanted to try, he got.

He hasn't had time to check his bank account. If you ask him when the last time he checked his balance was, I'm sure he wouldn't have an answer. He's confident that his inheritance will never run out, no matter how he's using it.

The time comes when he's hungry, he needs to eat, he needs to regain his strength so he can continue having fun.

He wants to use his bank card, but it's declined.

His balance doesn't cover what he wants to spend this time.

It must be a mistake, he must've thought. The inheritance should last forever.

He needs to go to the bank to sort out this misunderstanding.

And he is met with the shock that this inheritance has been squandered.

His balance is zero.

The hunger he feels is not helping him think clearly.

Without money in the account, what will he eat now?

We have been discussing the inheritance of this young man and how he has wasted it; it's time to go into detail. If we put ourselves in the place of this young man representing humanity, what is our inheritance that we have squandered?

In the previous section, we saw how the father of the two sons, while on the estate, stands in front of them and extends his two hands. In one of them, he holds his brain, his knowledge.

In the other hand, he holds his heart, connection, relationship. We, as humanity, prefer to take from knowledge, from the brain, and walk away with what we believe will help us excel, to be like him.

We don't want to be his image; we don't want to be his shadow; we want to be defined by ourselves.

In the other hand is where the true inheritance lies. It's the connection with the father.

A connection from our spirit to his. Relationship, communication, purpose.

When Adam and Eve were inside the estate, the paradise, they had that connection with God. Their priority was his company, just being with him and spending time together, in relationship.

Inside there, they could eat from the fruit of the trees. Every fruit they found inside the garden they could eat, including the tree of life, which would keep them alive and healthy. As long as they continued eating from that fruit, they would maintain that relationship.

Except from the tree of knowledge, because they didn't need it.

Knowing that you are much more than a body of flesh wandering through this world gives you a purpose, or at least pushes you to seek one.

Knowing that we are much more than an animal that evolved makes us search for the reason why we are in this world; without it, we are just wandering, feeding on what we find, or on what others think we should eat.

And that's what happened with Adam and Eve. When they decided to take the inheritance and leave, that connection broke. They no longer saw themselves as spiritual beings but became aware of the body they were in, and their priorities changed. Now they would have to cover their nakedness to feed that new feeling called shame.

Now they would have to eat what they found, and if they wanted to taste different fruits that reminded them of life within the estate, they would have to work the land to get them.

Now it would cost them the sweat of their brow to have a glimpse of what they ate when they had that connection.

How do you nourish yourself after you have squandered your inheritance?

When you are hungry for self-esteem, when you are hungry for protection, for security, for improvement...

And you check your bank account where you had your inheritance, and your balance is zero.

And you go to cut the fruit from the tree of life that will make you feel much better and will let you know that you are much more than a body of flesh resulting from an accident, and you only find the stump of the tree where the roots join. What do you eat then?

Do you remember the previous section? King Nebuchadnezzar had a dream where he saw a tree that connected the earth and the sky, and the tree was cut down because the king believed he was the most significant character in his life.

But among all this, hope was given. The stump of the tree was left, where the roots join, as a sign that once that tree existed. And it was told to him that the day he looked up and recognized that there is a God, then this tree would be restored, and he would become a human being again (Daniel 4).

God gave King Nebuchadnezzar time. He let him know in his dream that the roots were still there, waiting for him to decide to return, until he decided to look up to the sky and recognize God.

At this moment, the prodigal son has the option to return to his father and apologize, to state his case and surrender to whatever the father's decision may be.

He doesn't know how his father will take it, or if he will take him back after he decided to become emancipated.

The young man had no idea what was going through the father's head at that moment. But we are given a glimpse of what God thinks when we are in those moments of hunger...

"I will go and return to my place until they acknowledge their sin and seek my face. In their distress, they will seek me" (Hosea 5:15).

God speaking, saying that in those moments of distress, those moments of hunger, he is like a father in a waiting room, pacing back and forth, thinking:

He's going to look at me, he's going to return to me.

And while we are thinking about what decision to make, he keeps pacing back and forth, waiting for us.

Before acting in desperation, before doing things guided by instincts, and before asking the question: where was God when this was happening?

God is giving us the answer to that question. He says he is waiting for us to look up, to seek him, that he is just waiting for us to recognize him so he can accept us again.

For that reason, he left the stump of the tree within us, to remind us that we are much more than just a bad moment, much more than a wrong decision.

This would have been the perfect moment in the story of the prodigal son for him to reach into his pocket and find a credit card that would give him hope during this time of hunger. But that didn't happen.

The good news is that we are given one: knowing that God is waiting for us, that he is watching us, but at the end of the day, the choice is ours.

The prodigal son has in his mind the image of his father's estate, with all the comforts he used to enjoy.

But in the distance, in front of him, he can see another estate, with another owner, a new territory...

Decisions, decisions...

Chapter 12
Identity or ID Entity

> *"How many of my father's hired servants have food to spare, and here I am starving to death!"*
> (Luke 15:17)

> *"Where do wars and fights come from among you? Do they not come from your desires for pleasure that war in your members?"*
> (James 4:1)

It has been a long journey. The younger son has seen various places, experienced things different from what he knew, and witnessed many new sights.

The inheritance he received from his father has been squandered. He has nothing left of those riches, nothing left to remind him of where he comes from.

As soon as he lost all his belongings, it seems he also lost the purpose for which he was in that distant land. He was supposed to have gone there to enjoy, to vacation, but at this moment, he's not enjoying his stay there.

It seems that money was not the only thing he lost because he no longer sees himself as a visitor or vacationer. Now, he sees himself as someone who belongs to that place and, therefore, must fulfill a role in that society or entity.

The decisions he will make now will be based on his experience or how he sees himself.

He is ready to apply for a job. If he still has the clothing he wore when he left his father's estate, it might help him during the interview. If not, he'll have to make a greater effort to persuade his potential employer, as part of the interview will be judged based on his appearance.

Having lived his entire life on an estate, he is familiar with the system there. So, the most logical step for him now would be to look for a job on another estate. As the son of an estate owner, I imagine that even though he's young, he must have spent time with his father, watching and learning how to manage the estate. Asking his father questions about the system, preparing for the time when he would become the new manager.

If this wasn't the case, he's likely in a tight spot. On the job application, where one needs to specify the desired position, the roles of manager or supervisor might seem too big for him based on his experience, or lack thereof. Perhaps, had he mentioned he was the son of an estate owner, they would have considered him for a position where he could leverage that influence or identity. But it seems he even forgot who he was and didn't think to mention it.

The person hiring, based on this young man's experience, assigns him the task of feeding the pigs. This is his new role on this estate, his new identity. From being the son of the owner, he's now the one who feeds the pigs. This is the label given to him, based on his experience, his knowledge, and more than anything, his desperation to belong to an entity. To be part of the group of people who had a role within the estate.

Now, all his focus and energy would have to be used to perform this new role.

Now, this young man has a new answer to the question: "Who are you?"

To answer this question, we must have certain beliefs about ourselves. These beliefs might be based on our roles in society, such as our gender, race, religion, surname, or some profession or career that we have studied or are practicing. Or perhaps our answer is based on character traits or behavioral tendencies, such as being social, optimistic, religious, or conservative.

The difference is that if your identity is based more on your societal roles, there's a danger that when one of these roles is at risk or changes, we could face an identity crisis.

For instance, if someone bases their identity on their role as a spouse, and after many years, for whatever reason, they lose their partner, now their role changes, either to that of a divorcee or a widow/widower. The role or persona on which they based their identity is removed, and this individual finds themselves in an identity crisis, seeking something to fill that void.

If we don't have a defined identity, if we don't have defined values or ethics, we will fall into collective morality. This morality is based on what we see around us, on what we observe others doing, and since others are doing it, we're not the only one, which makes this behavior or attitude common.

It becomes the new concept of "normal."

On one occasion, Jesus was on a boat with his disciples; in fact, this occurred after the storm I mentioned in chapter 9 when Jesus was sleeping in the boat. They arrived on the other side of the lake, at a place called Gadara. There was a man living in the cemetery there; the way he's described makes him seem quite the spectacle.

He lived among the tombs, walking around naked. Every time they tried to bind him, even with chains, he broke them. He spent his days and nights in the cemetery, shouting and hurting himself. No one could subdue him (Mark 5:1-20).

Although no one could control him, and attempts to do so had failed, it seems the inhabitants of that region had grown accustomed to him. I think the fact that they had someone nearby who was in a much worse situation made them feel that they weren't as bad off as they thought:

In their moments of anger, they could say: at least I'm not shouting on the mountains.

When they felt their clothes were dirty, they could remind themselves: at least I'm not naked.

If they had an accident due to negligence, there was someone who hurt himself on purpose.

If they didn't eat as well as they wanted that day, there was someone eating grass.

If they felt their house wasn't as elegant as their neighbors', they knew of someone who lived in the tombs.

If they felt burdened with problems, there was someone dragging chains.

They had someone who was in a much worse situation than they were.

They had someone with whom they could compare themselves and think that they weren't in such a dire situation.

They had someone on whom they could project any label that society wanted to place on them.

Someone who made them appear normal.

Jesus didn't see things the same way they did, and he had what this person needed. So, he freed him from this spiritual situation, which was the root of his behavior.

If what the inhabitants of that region wanted was a spectacle, they witnessed one that day: a man being freed from a legion of demons.

How did the people in that place react to this?

> *"They came to Jesus and saw the one who had been demon-possessed, who had the legion, sitting, clothed, and in his right mind; and they were afraid."*
> (Mark 5:15).

When this person was troubled, they had the courage to approach him, to put more chains on him, to bind him further, to label him, to give him new nicknames.

To remind him of how bad he was.

Now that they see him transformed, at their level, and that he can look them in the eye, they feel fear. This was not normal for them.

They're not afraid of the person, but afraid of having to confront their own problems, afraid of facing themselves. Because now they have no one else to label but themselves.

"It shouldn't be this way," they think.

The same happened with the prodigal son; he was in the pigsty, feeding the pigs.

The pigs were eating, and he was starving.

> *He longed to fill his stomach with the pods that the pigs were eating, BUT NO ONE GAVE HIM ANYTHING.*
> (Luke 15:16).

When one is hungry, instincts are exposed; for they will seek to feed that area of our life that is suffering at the moment, be it self-esteem, security, the sexual area, or self-improvement; instincts are capable of anything for satisfaction.

If these people had given the prodigal son some pods, it would have satisfied him momentarily, quelling that instinct. The best thing for them was not to give him what he needed and wait for the moment when this instinct would come to the surface, making the young man act irrationally; this would give them the opportunity to see someone doing something they would "never fall into".

That's one of the problems with accepting the label or identity that other people give you.

That's one of the problems with forgetting who you are.

If the prodigal son, in his new job, had seen many more people doing the same task, maybe he wouldn't have been bothered or wouldn't have cared about continuing what he was doing.

But if he's the only person doing that task, then he's going to feel labeled.

He's going to feel uncomfortable, and that's going to bring questions or doubts about his identity.

Identity based on your role in society looks outward, and it can be changed or manipulated by something or someone else.

Identity based on your character looks inward, and this gives you control to change the situation you are in.

The identity you embrace today is what you will become.

Chapter 13
You Are Here
(Reflection)

When you go to the mall, and you're looking for a specific store, or you don't know where to go, there's a map of the place at certain parts of the mall with an icon or pointer that shows you where you're standing so you know where to head next. This icon is labeled: you are here.

When you're driving and suddenly find yourself in an unfamiliar place, what you do is open the map on your phone or GPS, and it will show you an icon so you know exactly your location. Once you know where you stand, you'll know where to go to reach your destination.

When my son was in elementary school, I used to drop him off in the mornings, and at the school's entrance, I'd tell him: you are here. And since you're here, you can't be anywhere else. If you're here, focus on what you're doing. If you're here, it's to learn. Once you leave here, you'll be home and then you can focus on other things. But for now: you are here.

I know it sounds very obvious, what I've just written, but even I use this when I'm in different places or situations during the day. If I'm at home, I can't be anywhere else, so I can't be using my energy, thinking about a situation that will happen tomorrow when I get to work.

When I leave work, I know I'm not there anymore. I need to focus and dedicate myself to whatever I am doing at that moment. Everything starts with knowing where you are, and owning that. All we have is now; wherever you were yesterday or a week ago is just a memory. We can learn from what occurred then and apply it today to avoid making the same mistakes.

We can imagine the next week and make plans or set appointments. We can visualize ourselves two years ahead and set goals for that time, preparing ourselves for when that moment comes. One thing we cannot deny is our current situation or condition. The decisions we've made have brought us here. The only person who got you to where you are now is you.

We can be manipulated, we can be convinced, but ultimately, we make the decisions. We accept what others offer us, or we reject it and choose to go our own way. You can blame whomever you want for your current situation or condition. However, the undeniable truth is that regardless of who you blame, the only person responsible for getting out of it is you. The only people who benefit from leaving that situation are ourselves.

We'll always have the option to blame someone else, of course. But making that choice won't move us from where we stand; we'll remain stuck in the same situation. We can spend all our energy trying to convince and explain to ourselves how we got there, but that still won't move us out of that spot.

No matter what situation or condition you find yourself in. It doesn't matter how far away you are from the store you want to visit inside the mall. Similarly, when you're lost on the road and the phone or GPS shows you how far you are from where you planned to go. That's just the starting point, where we need to begin. If we are far from home, that's just point A. It's just our location. Nothing more.

The prodigal son has lost his identity. He has lost his inheritance. He has lost his purpose. He stands in a pigsty, surrounded by pigs that seemingly eat better than he does. It doesn't matter anymore how he got there. That's just point A. That's just where he needs to start. It's just where we need to start. You are here.

Chapter 14
Camel's Heart

> *"And coming to his senses, he said: 'How many hired servants of my father's have bread enough and to spare, and I perish here with hunger!'"*
> (Luke 15:17)

> *"And I saw him, and I have borne witness that this is the Son of God."*
> (John 1:34)

Some time ago, during those moments when I question myself, there was one question that prompted me to seek the opinions of others for an answer. The question is: why are there religious or spiritual people and others for whom this topic doesn't seem to be a priority?

We have been discussing identity to find answers, or to pave the way for better answers. We must ask ourselves: who am I?

As I mentioned in Chapter 12, we must have a concept of ourselves to find an identity. These concepts can be based on our relationship with others or our role in society. Alternatively, they can be based on something deeper, like traits of our character.

But for this other question, I had to dig a bit deeper, and the question I posed to several people was: what are you?

Some preferred not to answer.

Others said they were flesh.

Others said they are products of evolution.

Others believed they are animals with a higher mental development.

Yet others said they were humans. Which led me to the question: what defines a human? The answer given was: my physical complexion or form.

The answer we have to this question will help, or in some ways, dictate how we react in our daily lives.

But if we were to ask this to John the Baptist, what would he answer?

John the Baptist was a prophet. Before Jesus began his ministry, John spent his time at the Jordan River, baptizing people who came to him. He recounts that when he received God's call to be the Baptist, he was given a sign by which he would recognize who the Christ would be. He was told that upon whom he saw the Holy Spirit descend like a dove and rest upon, that person would be the Christ. It couldn't be more specific than that.

John lived in the desert. The Bible mentions that he was clothed in camel's skin. Camel skin has thermostatic properties; in the heat, it keeps the camel cool, and in the cold, it provides protection. Thus, while dressed in this skin, John could endure time in the desert, as if it helped him adapt to the climatic conditions.

One day, Jesus came to him to be baptized. John baptized him, and lo and behold, a dove descended and rested upon Jesus.

John himself proclaimed, "I saw him, this is the Son of God." (John 1:34). There was no room for doubt. He was convinced.

Another thing John the Baptist was convinced of was his own identity. Shortly before Jesus was baptized, some people sent by the religious authorities came to question him about why he was baptizing people. They asked him, "Who are you? What do you say about yourself?" (John 1:22).

On that occasion, John replied with a prophecy from the book of Isaiah, which pointed towards him:

"I am the voice of one calling in the wilderness: 'Make straight the way for the Lord.'" (Isaiah 40:3).

His mission was to prepare the way, to ready the people for the coming of the Messiah. John the Baptist declared: "I was born to live in the desert and to baptize. That is who I am."

As time passed, Herod, one of the rulers of that region, had John the Baptist imprisoned. John was no longer in the desert, no longer baptizing, and people no longer came to him. Now he was John the Prisoner.

He had based his entire identity on his role as a prophet, as well as his lifestyle of living in the desert and baptizing. But what happens when he's moved from the desert and stripped of the chance to fulfill his role? Now he's confined, with no one coming to him. That camel-skin coat, which had so helped him adapt to the conditions, seems unable to do much for him now. His identity is at risk.

Why do I think this? It turns out that while John was in prison, he sent two of his disciples to ask Jesus a question: "Are you the one who is to come, or should we expect someone else?" (Matthew 11:3).

While John was baptizing and living in the desert, he would say: I know that Jesus is the chosen one. When things didn't go as he expected, he wondered: could Jesus be the chosen one?

We all have a camel-skin coat that helps us adapt to the conditions in our daily life, whether it's our IQ, position, influence, salary, charisma, savings account, social circle, etc. There will be times when none of these will help us define our identity. And like John, we will not only doubt ourselves but also our very beliefs.

How can that coat help us when the cold and darkness do not come from the night, but from within us? How does it help us when the scorching heat does not come from the sun, but from our worries, frustration, and doubts? How does it help when the loneliness of the desert has nothing to do with the number of people surrounding you, but how you feel inside?

When everything contrary comes from within oneself, not only do we need a camel-skin coat, we need a camel's heart, a heart that helps us adapt to the circumstances and conditions in our lives.

Throughout the day, we are changing identities depending on what we are doing, where we are, or even depending on the people who are around us at that moment. For instance, when I'm at home with my family, I am a father, a husband, a protector, and a provider. When I leave for work and am on my way, I am a responsible citizen abiding by traffic laws.

When I get to my job, I am an employee of that place, with rules to follow and roles to fulfill. But of all the identities we can exercise in a day, there's one that stands out the most: our identity of origin.

This is the identity that, when we see it's at risk, we experience frustration. That's why when we're at school and our parents come to visit, the atmosphere feels a bit strange, as you're both a student and a child at the same time. Or when we're at work and our family visits – you're a parent while in your workplace. Or when a colleague from work visits us at home. Two identities are clashing to take precedence at that moment.

Thus, we need an identity that goes with us all the time, regardless of where we are.

This brings me to the question I asked at the beginning of the chapter: what are you?

Let me share my answer to that question: I am a spirit within a body. Immaterial clothed in matter. A spirit that transcends time, the circumstances of each day, and even death.

Identifying yourself in this way will help you see things differently, even in the way you behave and see others because you now understand that they too are a spirit within a body. Identifying yourself this way will help you find a purpose, because you know there's much more beyond this world, the spirit continues even after death. Identifying yourself in this manner will also help you realize that God will always see you the same way.

When John the Baptist was in jail, since his identity was tied to a prophecy made about him, the fact that he wasn't exercising his foundational identity placed him in a position of frustration, leading him to doubt not only himself but also Jesus. However, even when he sent messengers to question Jesus about His identity, once they left to return to John, Jesus made clear that he still regarded John in the same light (Luke 7:26-28). Jesus turned to the crowd around him and proclaimed, "John is a prophet, and there is none born like him."

While John was in the desert, Jesus remained the same. While John was imprisoned, Jesus remained unchanged. In the desert, in the darkness, in the cold, Jesus remains consistent.

God is unchanging. Thus, an identity that ties or connects you with Him will help you remain consistent no matter your circumstances or where you find yourself. If we root our identity in God, He remains steadfast.

The prodigal son stands in the mud, feeding pigs, reflecting on his fallen state. He looks around and sees no one but the animals; he's alone. In his heart, he sees himself as a mere laborer. He looks up to the blazing sun, with no protection against it.

Far away, on another estate, his father gazes at the same sun, wondering how his departed son is faring. They're physically distant but emotionally connected, each thinking of the other.

And for the first time in a long while, the younger son remembers that he has a father, that he belongs to something much bigger than his current dire circumstances.

And he remembers he is a son.

"In my father's house... My father?... My father!"

And at the stump, where the roots come together, where once there was a tree connecting heaven and earth, a sprout starts to appear. It's time to return.

Chapter 15
Closing One's Eyes

> *I will arise and go to my father, and will say to him: Father, I have sinned against heaven and before you.*
> (Luke 15:18)

> *Then the eyes of both of them were opened, and they realized they were naked; so they sewed fig leaves together and made themselves loincloths.*
> (Genesis 3:7)

When Adam and Eve ate of the fruit they were told not to eat, the first thing they experienced was that their eyes were opened.

The word used in Hebrew for this verse is PACAKJ. Using this word in reference to the eyes has a more figurative meaning: it is to open one's senses, in this case, sight, to be more observant, a change in perception, a shift in the way one looks at their surroundings.

In their case, it seems that before eating the fruit, innocence or a lack of malice allowed them to focus on what they were: a spirit that had communication and a relationship with their father, their creator.

The nourishment they needed was right in front of them. The more they communicated with God, the more they became like Him. There was a connection, and their sustenance was that relationship.

When they ate from the tree of knowledge, the first thing they became aware of was that they were inside a fleshly body.

A body they now had to nourish, and I'm not referring to food but to needs, instincts that were coming to light.

Being aware that they were a body created limitations, caution.

They needed to know how far they could go with the body, its strength has a limit.

Now they knew fear, now they could be hurt, they felt pain.

This new perception brought about new feelings. Before eating the fruit, they walked naked in the garden. Once they tasted it, the shift in perception made them see each other's nakedness and they felt shame.

Before tasting the fruit, they saw each other as spirits in the garden.

Once they tasted it, their perception changed by the way they now looked at each other, one body looking at another.

One thing that caught my attention in this passage from Genesis 3, is the fact that when they looked at each other, they felt shame. But when they heard the voice of God in the garden and ran to hide, it wasn't out of shame, but out of fear (v. 10).

How could it be that after the connection and relationship they had, Adam now felt fear even thinking of God?

Could it be that seeing himself as a fleshly body made it more difficult for him to understand the spiritual world?

Is it that when you change your perception, when you open your eyes to a new world, your priorities change?

For this concept, there is a word that comes from Latin: numinous.

It's a very rare word, even as I wrote it, the computer was trying to correct me or offer more options in case

I intended to write something different.

This word is used to describe the presence of something that is outside our material world. The presence of a divine being, of a deity, something spiritual.

The word comes from the Latin *numen*: presence, deity, spirit.

And *nous*: intelligence, reason, mind.

It's as if you're trying to rationalize or understand something that is from another dimension.

You're in your bedroom in the middle of the night, suddenly you hear a noise in the kitchen; the first thing you think is that another family member is in the kitchen looking for something.

You hear the noise again, only this time, your mind reminds you that you're the only family member inside the house at that moment.

It's at that point where your mind tries to understand how, with no one else in the house, there's still activity being heard. Your consciousness, which operates based on reality, on reason, tries to make sense of what you're experiencing. It tries to rationalize to provide an explanation for the event.

Numinous becomes a feeling that the mind tries to be aware of, understand, or describe, and the only way it can do so is through emotions.

This process can make you feel two things: either you feel fear because you can't make sense of what you're witnessing, or you feel awe because you're in a situation outside your routine life.

These feelings can only be revealed depending on your perception, how you see life, how you see yourself.

Let me ask you another question: what do you feel when you think of God?

Do you feel fear like Adam and Eve when they heard His voice in the garden?

Do you feel shame because you feel naked before Him, and you don't want Him to see you for who you truly are?

Do you feel judged for whatever you have done with your life?

Do you feel He is unattainable?

Are you in awe to know that there is someone much greater than you?

Do you feel reverence knowing there's a creator whom you can get to know?

Do you feel that you're much more than a fleshly body when your environment is invaded by something spiritual?

When the prodigal son had spent all his inheritance and began to be hungry, there came a point when he had the choice to return to the estate, or to keep walking away from it.

Thinking of the father seemed to produce in him a feeling of shame, having to return empty-handed.

A feeling of failure, wanting to do what he wanted with his life, and look at me now.

He didn't want to be judged, to be seen by all the people who lived there?

Those feelings drove him further away, although those feelings had nothing to do with the father's reaction. It was solely the way he saw himself that made him think that way.

Once he saw himself at rock bottom and remembered he had a father.

What made him a son, his view of the father changed, and he remembered that he can approach Him, that he can speak with Him.

I will arise... and go... and tell him.

I will approach and speak to Him.

I can draw near.

When Adam and Eve tasted the fruit, their eyes were opened, and that made them move away from God, to see life in a different way, to see themselves as bodies of flesh.

If we close our eyes, and look within ourselves and search for that breath that God once blew into us, I am sure we will find the missing link that connects us to God, that makes us something much greater than what we believe we are now.

That spirit within us is the true link we must find.

Chapter 16
The Theory Of R-evolution

But because you are sons, God has sent forth the Spirit of His Son into your hearts, crying out, "Abba, Father!"
(Galatians 4:6)

And he released to them the one they requested, who for rebellion and murder had been thrown into prison; but he delivered Jesus to their will.
(Luke 23:25)

How do you react to circumstances?

What do you do when you disagree with something that is affecting you?

What's the next step when you're discontented or unsatisfied even with yourself?

Often, we react in ways that we don't even understand. After we do or say the first thing that comes to mind, we realize we hurt someone else or ourselves, our image, and we don't know why we did it.

We need to understand how we function, to know ourselves so that we can predict and prevent our reactions the next time we're in a situation demanding one from us.

The day of the Passover is approaching. While some are preparing to celebrate this festival, others are busy trying to get rid of a man who, according to them, is stirring up the people.

This man is Jesus; the chief priests and the people have agreed to ask the governor to help them get rid of him.

Pilate is in a dilemma, after questioning Jesus he realizes that he has done nothing wrong, he finds no fault in him.

On the other hand, he has the people and the priests pressuring him to do something about it.

There was a tradition in which the governor, around the day of the Passover, would release a prisoner. Among those who behaved best, one would be set free.

Pilate has a plan, this time he will do it differently, this time he will give them the choice between one of the prisoners and Jesus.

Pilate chooses a prisoner with a very bad reputation, very infamous, Barabbas.

We have the three characters standing at the tribunal.

The people and the priests in front of them.

Pilate, standing in the middle, will decide how this entanglement ends. (Or at least he believes so).

By his side is Jesus, who according to them, stirs up the people with strange doctrines.

On the other side is Barabbas, his reputation precedes him, murderer, thief, agitator.

When I see the three standing at the tribunal, I think:

How would each of them resolve a conflict?

How would they defend their position, their beliefs, how would they react?

If each of them had the opportunity to decide how to address their grievances.

Even better, if each of them could resolve your discomforts.

If there was something you'd like to change within you, a pattern, a habit.

And each of them lived inside your head, and you could go to each one to present your case, how do you think they would resolve it?

Even better, if I told you that each of them lives inside your head, and that every day, when you're in a stressful situation that requires action, you can go to each of them and ask them to solve it...

Barabbas:

Sedition. He's cold. If he's not satisfied with something, he will try to convince those around him that something is wrong, he will recruit more people to rise up in arms against the system.

He will do everything possible to show his discontent in a violent way, and along the way, if someone gets hurt, or if someone dies, it's just collateral damage, just to make a point, just to show discontent.

When something doesn't seem right to you, the first thing you do is share it with others to see if you're the only one who thinks that way; if you are the only one, at least you have already planted a seed in someone else's mind, just wait for it to germinate and bear fruit.

Perhaps someone else will join your cause.

If we have to hurt someone else to protect our interests, it's something that has to happen, we say.

If we have to act violently to be heard, or to show that something doesn't seem right to us, it has to be done that way, we say.

This Barabbas that makes us react in such a way within us is called instincts, impulses, flesh.

Pilate:

Reform. He is more calculating, first thinking: if he says or does something, how might it affect things?

In a reform, you choose the laws to be changed or modified and those that won't be.

You don't remove a system from power as in a sedition, but rather modify the laws partially so that everyone is satisfied.

Pilate might be aware that something is wrong, but if he works on that, someone else might be dissatisfied. One of Pilate's concerns is to be good with everyone, play the game so that everyone is satisfied, sometimes acting a role while the conflict passes.

Pilate knows what the truth is, but if everyone around thinks that the truth can be manipulated, then Pilate believes that collective truth or democracy (majority vote) can define what is true and what is not.

Pilate can rationalize his decisions to make himself believe that he is doing the right thing even though deep down he knows he isn't. This rationalization can brainwash him or, on occasions, wash his hands.

Even if Pilate knows the truth and is convinced by it, he can look the other way and pretend he knows nothing; perhaps ignoring or suppressing the problems will help them disappear.

This Pilate that makes us react this way within us is called reason, mind, self, soul.

Jesus:

Revolution. He has discontent, and he is willing to do something to change the system. But he also knows that in a revolution, to change something, you first have to change yourself in order to demonstrate the result and change others.

The person leading a revolution must be willing to give their life for that movement.

They must be willing to die to achieve that change.

Throughout history, individuals have started revolutions and have been willing to give their lives for what they believe in, and they have died for it. They may not have lived to see the change or result they were fighting for, but the people who believed in it and carried on with the revolution did see it.

That was what Jesus was doing, showing a different way of living, demonstrating that life could be better, that if you didn't just see yourself as a fleshly body walking through this world, but instead connected back with the father and acknowledged you are a spirit within that body, transcending all that's material, you'd find a purpose for living.

Jesus was convinced of this. In fact, on one occasion, he mentioned he was willing to give his life for what he believed in (John 10:18).

This Jesus that makes us react this way inside us is called integrity, morality, spirit.

Once we recognize and accept that we are children of God, He sends the spirit of His son into our hearts. This spirit will connect us with the father and will drive us to be more like Him every day. It will help us be less of ourselves and more like Him.

That's what's needed, a revolution—people who are willing to die for change, willing to die for their beliefs. When I talk about dying, I refer to dying to ourselves to achieve that change. We can't talk about change if we don't exemplify it ourselves.

A true revolution is when you find something you'd be willing to die for.

Even when we are no longer here, when someone remembers our name, may that memory point to God, point to the change we demonstrated during our life, and may this lead others to believe, to change, to follow this revolution.

Before Jesus was crucified for preaching that revolution, before being arrested, he was talking to his father, and he said:

"I have finished the work which you have given me to do, I have glorified your name" (John 17:4).

As if that was the purpose for which he came to earth, just to uplift God's name through his lifestyle.

Jesus believed it to be so, and he was willing to die for it.

I believe it too, and I am willing to give my life for it.

And you, would you be willing to die for what you believe in?

Chapter 17
Imperfect Past Tense
(Reflection)

"If I had... if only I had."
The prodigal son has risen from where he
was, and has begun to walk back.
He had to quit his job, he had to accept
that he is a son, not a laborer.
He knows that it was his decisions that led him to where he
was, he realized that emancipation is not as easy as he thought.
He could have done things differently, he could
have said things in a different way.
In his head, there are countless scenarios, of
everything that he could have changed.
If he hadn't been so aggressive when he asked
for his share of the inheritance.
If he had used different terms so as not to make his father
believe that he wanted nothing to do with him.
If he had paid more attention to how an estate is
managed, maybe he would have gotten a better job.
If he hadn't rushed so much, he wouldn't have spent
the inheritance in such a short time.

That's why the expression "hubiera" (would have) is known as the imperfect past tense, because it never happened that way, we can only wish for different outcomes, but the reality is different.
We can only torture ourselves with
different scenarios inside our minds.

Scenarios that never occurred. The difference between thinking things and doing or saying them is that you can take back a thought, at the end of the day it remains only between you and your mind. But a word or action, once released, cannot be taken back.

What makes our past or our "pretérito" imperfect is the continuous desire to go back and change things that already happened. It's the ongoing torture over what we said or did.

The moment we acknowledge what we said or did, the moment we realize we can't turn back time, the moment we own up to our actions and take responsibility for them, the moment we say: I did it, I said it, our past becomes perfect.

Because recognizing our actions is just the beginning of starting to change. If we keep denying it or blaming someone else, we haven't learned anything and are prone to make the same mistake again.

Once we recognize what we did and take responsibility for it, that's being accountable. Being responsible simply means, if someone asks you why you did what you did, and you can answer that question, then you're responsible. If you can explain the reasons behind your actions, you are accountable.

Once we take responsibility for our actions, we can own our past and learn from it. That will help us respond better in the future.

The night before, the prodigal son told himself he would get up and go to his father. Now he is on his way. He has a phrase in his mind: I have sinned. Yes, I did it.

I'm coming back to face the consequences.
Living away doesn't improve the situation.
These scenarios in my mind aren't helping me.
Dreaming of different ways to handle things doesn't let me close this chapter in my life.
Yes, I did it.
The night before it was a... I will go to my father.
Today it's... I'm on my way.
Yes, I am doing it.

Chapter 18
Intersections

> *"And he arose and came to his father. But when he was still a great way off, his father saw him and had compassion, and ran and fell on his neck and kissed him."*
> (Luke 15:20)

> *"And being found in appearance as a man, He humbled Himself and became obedient to the point of death, even the death of the cross."*
> (Philippians 2:8)

It's a new day; the prodigal son has decided to return. He has looked within himself and has recognized that he made a mistake. He has observed his condition and knows that he lost his identity in that venture he undertook.

As he makes his way, he has time to think about what he will say, time to rehearse his apology speech. On one hand, he hopes that the father will forgive him. That's all he desires, a place to sleep. A place he can call home. A place to belong.

On the other hand, he doesn't expect to regain his title as a son or its benefits. He just wants a job as a day laborer. To earn his bread and a place to rest.

The journey is long, and the only thing he can do to improve the situation is to approach the father again and leave everything in his hands. How he would give anything to be able to change the father's mind and be sure of what will happen.

He walks along the side of the road, trying to trace the way back to the estate.

After some time, he approaches the estate. He can see it from a distance.

Anxiety tries to overtake his thoughts, showing him various scenarios where the situation doesn't end as he hopes...

What if they don't let you in...

What if the father decides he doesn't want you back...

What if the father doesn't recognize you...

His steps become slower, he needs more time to think.

Near the estate, there's an intersection where two roads cross.

One road ends at the gate of the estate, the other just runs alongside it.

He stops at the intersection, looks both ways to make sure he can cross.

Then he looks forward, he can see the entrance to the estate.

He goes over his apology speech again. He hopes that this speech will grant him a place to return to, nothing will be the same, but he will be back.

In fact, what the son was offering was to live in the same place, but without a relationship, like employer and employee, they didn't have to interact much.

This reminds me of chapter four when humanity is mentioned trying to build a door to heaven, Babel.

Instead of seeking God, they wanted to find the entrance to heaven themselves so they could visit whenever they wanted.

There's no way to find or build an entrance to heaven without a relationship or a connection with God himself. It's absurd to think that we can earn a place there through our merits or actions.

The highest we can reach to find that door is by being raised on a cross.

Jesus himself said that if he were lifted up, he would draw everyone to him, speaking of the cross (John 12:32-33).

There's a point where the father and son will meet.

An intersection where two lives will intersect.

If you don't go through that intersection, you can't get to the door.

That cross is the lowest place God could reach.

That cross is the highest place we can reach.

That's where we will meet.

An intersection before the entrance to the estate.

In the story of the prodigal son, the father waits at the estate for the son to decide to return.

In our story, the father decides to rise from his throne and come looking for us on earth.

In the story of the prodigal son, we see the father who sees the son from a distance and recognizes him.

For a person with the father's position at the estate, seeing him run would be an awkward act for everyone around.

The father didn't care if others saw him run.

In our story, the father not only ran towards us but became one of us, left his position to come for us.

In the story of the prodigal son, the father didn't care that the son came dirty and smelly; he still approached him and embraced him.

In our story, the father did much more than that; he chose to get dirty by bearing all our sins, by bearing the curse of being hung on the cross.

In the story of the prodigal son, the father accepted the son just as he was, he didn't judge him for his appearance, or the condition he was in...

The only "BUT" the father had was when the son told him he didn't deserve to be his son.

Just to emphasize that he didn't feel the same way, just to show that he thinks differently.

That we can't use our biases to label him thinking he'd react like one of us.

The "BUT" the father brings up is to tell him he thinks differently.

Just to emphasize that he was his son, and the son accepted what the father told him. He allowed himself to be embraced, allowed himself to be accepted, allowed himself to be adopted as a son once again.

In our story, the only "BUT" is the one we place ourselves.

Chapter 19
Heaven and Earth Kiss

> *"And he arose, and came to his father. But when he was yet a great way off, his father saw him, and had compassion, and ran, and fell on his neck, and kissed him."*
> (Luke 15:20)

> *Mercy and truth have met each other;*
> *Justice and peace have kissed.*
> (Psalms 85:10)

Let's go back to the moment when the son stands at the intersection. His head is filled with doubts about the father's reaction.

He might look for a way to explain what happened, painting himself as the victim of his impulses.

Victim of curiosity, even of ignorance.

This is what we do most of the time when we do something wrong; we try to see ourselves as victims to soften the punishment or consequences.

We are good at defending ourselves and deflecting blame onto something or someone else.

Instead of the prodigal son, we might have blamed the father for being too strict with us.

Or the pressure of the estate was too much; it was overwhelming me, so I had to run away.

Our defense mechanisms would have been triggered in such a way that the father would have been the one who ended up apologizing.

But the prodigal son has no tricks up his sleeve.

The prodigal son only comes with one explanation: the truth.

I thought I could take the inheritance and enjoy exploring.

I thought the inheritance would last me longer.

I believed I could handle my life away from you.

I did wrong. It was a very poor decision.

He knew what he had done, and he acknowledged it.

And he was ready to face the consequences.

He takes a minute.

The time has come to cross the gate of the estate.

From a distance, he sees a figure coming towards him. He focuses his sight, and recognizes it; it's his father.

The father is running. The fact that the father has forgotten his position to run in front of his employees, for them to see him do that, must mean the father has lost control.

The entire estate and its surroundings found out what his own son did: he took half of his belongings and squandered them.

Now everyone will see him return with nothing, seeking refuge in the estate. The father must be very upset, to the point of running.

The son knows that what he did has consequences, and he must face them.

He knows he deserves punishment, and he is ready to receive it.

That's the concept of justice, giving each one what they deserve according to their actions.

The father has come close enough for the two of them to look into each other's eyes.

The son lowers his gaze to the ground and starts the conversation: I have sinned...

I am not worthy...

There's a confession.

There's enough evidence.

His appearance and clothing tell the story.

Even his own gaze could judge him.

The son is ready to receive the beating of his life...

The father has enough reasons to punish him, even to send him away.

In that moment, the father is the judge, the jury, and the executioner. He has all the power to make whatever decision comes to his mind, any punishment would be just.

Justice and truth face to face.

Of all the things the son expected, he received the least expected, what he never thought could be on his list of punishments: a hug.

Where are the punishments? Where are the insults?

Where are the "what have you done"? Where are the "how dare you"?

Where are the complaints? Where are the bills to pay?

The employees and those living in the estate take a break to appreciate this scene.

And more than appreciating, they try to understand what's happening.

Justice is supposed to give him what he deserves.

So, what is this called?

What do you call giving someone what they DON'T deserve?

According to the dictionary, there is a word that describes this; it's called grace, mercy.

The son doesn't understand this concept, even though he's experiencing it.

The son is looking at grace in the face.

He is hearing grace: "you are my son."

He is breathing grace, as he hears those words.

The only person who could judge and punish him thinks he's innocent.

The only person holding the evidence that could send anyone to life imprisonment chooses to erase the evidence.

The father chooses to ignore the fact that the son comes from afar with his dirty clothes and smelling of a pigsty.

And if you want this story to become even more irrational... The father gives him a kiss on the cheek.

As the son became more and more disfigured, as he lost his identity even more, the punishment became more severe; there was no way the son could justify what he did.

So, the father had to evolve his justice into grace.

In the story of the prodigal son, the father forgets everything the son did and justifies him, calling him innocent.

In our story, the father became flesh and took the beating for us.

He took the punishment for us; he took the curse for us.

If we can't call that grace, then I don't know what it is.

We cannot label God based on our system of justice.

We cannot label God based on our way of thinking, because that will only push us further away from Him.

With God, the way to face His justice is with the truth, a confession, accepting what we did, and surrendering to His verdict.

In this way, His justice becomes grace. He knows that we can never justify ourselves.

It doesn't matter how good we think we are at constructing arguments.

We cannot build a tower so high with our arguments to approach the Father and believe that we can be at His level.

We cannot build a door to heaven that we can open and enter whenever we want.

We cannot impress God, much less make Him feel guilty for our own decisions.

All that remains for us is to accept the truth, and surrender to His verdict.

He does not think like us. He does not judge like us.

By accepting this grace, the anxiety within us about how

He sees us fades away, and all this anxiety turns into peace, peace between Him and us.

This grace is the kiss with which God seals our adoption as His children.

The people around you will be trying to understand this scene.

But the only way to understand it is by opening your arms and experiencing it.

Chapter 20
Standing in Front of the Estate

> *"They shall make a sanctuary for me, and I will dwell among them."*
> (Exodus 25:8)

> *"No man of the descendants of Aaron the priest, who has a defect, shall come near to offer the offerings made by fire to the Lord. There is a defect in him; he shall not come near to offer the bread of his God."*
> (Leviticus 21:21)

Imagine the prodigal son returns to the estate, but sees that it has been remodeled. He stands in front of the estate, and from where he stands, he can see that his favorite places where he used to spend time are no longer there, or they are located somewhere else. The estate looks different; even the entrance has changed.

He would be confused, needing someone to guide him or show him the new way to reach his destination. He would have to explore the estate again to familiarize himself with the new paths, entries, exits, and determine where each door leads—everything is different.

This didn't happen in the parable of the prodigal son, but it did happen to humanity when they wanted to return and find God once more.

When Adam and Eve left paradise and passed through the gate, every subsequent generation continued moving eastward, distancing themselves further from paradise (recall that the only entrance to paradise was to the east).

Generations later, humanity wanted to return to God, and God decided to create something reminiscent of paradise, a place that would feel like home. So, He gave Moses the plans to build such a place, calling it the tabernacle. A place for living (for God), a dwelling place.

To enter this sanctuary, individuals had to undergo a process or preparation to stand before the Father. Notably, this tabernacle had only one entrance, and it faced east. Thus, anyone wishing to approach the tabernacle had to journey back from the east.

God was very specific when He spoke to Moses about the construction of this place. Materials, dimensions, colors—all were detailed, and the tabernacle had to be built in this prescribed manner.

The first time around, God gave man just one condition, and man failed to uphold it. He created man in His image, making him perfect. Yet, humanity did not want to mirror anyone. Instead, we preferred being the lead character in our own story.

Now, if humanity decided to return to Him, it would have to be on His terms. There were now intermediaries between God and man, individuals chosen by God to intercede on behalf of both parties. A process had been established that one needed to follow to ensure that God would accept the offering or sacrifice being presented.

Now there was a price to pay for every action, a sacrifice to offer, something to give in seeking forgiveness and reconciliation with God. It wasn't like before when they were expelled from paradise. It wasn't the same since the son left the estate.

Now there were sacrifices, offerings, conditions, and even a written book containing all the rules that needed to be followed and the conditions to be met to access the father. In fact, according to that rulebook, one had to be perfect to access the father.

Even if the priest, the person chosen to intercede, didn't comply with just one rule, he couldn't access God. He couldn't help anyone draw closer to God.

It was as if, previously, the younger son had access to the father's room, could enter and converse with him. Now, that room had become an office, and there were other offices you'd need to pass through before reaching the door to this one. Now, access depended on paperwork, appointments, conditions, even the dress code to present oneself before the father.

Imagine the son's frustration, going through all of that just to see his father. No matter how urgent the son's concern was, he had to relay his message to someone else, so that this person, who had access to the father that day, could convey the son's message.

When humanity wanted to reconnect with God, they believed it would be as simple as building a tower so tall it reached the heavens. They thought that, upon its completion, they could climb to its top and find God there, perhaps believing they could converse with Him at that height.

Using something material to access the immaterial world. Building a door to lead them to the spiritual realm, and just by naming it Babel, it would already become the door to God.

When God decided to reconnect with humanity, He communicated with Moses to show him how to access this immaterial world. Yes, there was a door, a curtain in fact, that provided access to the tabernacle, but this was just the beginning. Beyond it, one would encounter a multitude of rituals, sacrifices, and methods that had to be followed in order to access God.

One of the most important things before engaging with the tabernacle was the attitude with which you did it.

> *"God is Spirit, and those who worship Him must worship in spirit and truth."*
> (John 4:24).

You were about to enter the spiritual world to interact with God. But to enter the spiritual realm, you must become "spirit." You must understand that you are a spirit within a body. You need to modify the concept you have of yourself.

Every action inside the tabernacle, every utensil, every piece of furniture, every figure, every color, every measurement, all of it has symbolism. Everything makes sense. Everything has a purpose. However, in this book, I don't want to focus too much on the symbolism of the tabernacle. There are already many books that can explain that better.

I want to focus on how all of this applies to our lives, what we can take from it and apply to our daily lives that can help us understand God's purpose in our life... or maybe understand the purpose of our life.

The prodigal son has returned. The father has accepted him. But even for the son to enter the house, modifications must be made. Not for the son to be accepted, as he already was. But to enter the house, in front of the crowd who knew his story. He needed to be washed, put on a new garment, be given footwear, a ring. The people inside the house expected to see a son. And that's exactly what the father wanted them to see.

Are you ready to come in?

Section 3
The Return Home

Chapter 21
The Predestined Calf

> *"And bring the fattened calf to kill and eat..."*
> (Luke 15:23)

> *But with the precious blood of Christ, as of a lamb without blemish and without spot, foreordained before the foundation of the world, but made manifest in these last times for your sake.*
> (1 Peter 1:19-20)

We stand before the tabernacle. The only entrance is on the eastern side, where there's a large curtain. Inside, only the priests are allowed, who act as mediators between God and humans.

If they open the curtain and you're allowed to look, the first thing you'll see is an altar made of wood and covered in bronze. Square, a little over 2.2 meters wide and almost 1.4 meters high.

On this altar, the sacrifices people brought to appease or reconcile with God were burned.

If you commit a sin that's written in the book of Moses' law, right there it tells you the type of sacrifice you must bring to be forgiven.

It reminds you of why you're peeking into the tabernacle; you're there to offer a sacrifice. You bring your animal with you, which, by the way, has to be perfect. No kind of defect is accepted; it's an offense to bring something like that.

Before handing the animal to the priest, you stand in front of the animal and place your hand on its head, as if identifying with it. At that moment, this animal becomes your substitute; it will take your place, it will pay for what you did.

The elder son knows what we're talking about, the older brother of the prodigal son who stayed at home. He knows what it's like to work hard to please the father. He spends time in the field working to earn his father's favor.

When the prodigal son returned home, the elder brother was in the field. When he came back from work, he realized they were celebrating. The father came out to persuade him to join the party to celebrate his brother who had returned, but he refused.

His only claim was:

"Why did you give him the calf we've been fattening for a special occasion?"

Apparently, there was a calf they had designated for an occasion or an event that required a large meal. That calf was special.

The elder son had not had the opportunity to do something that would earn him enough credit to warrant the death of that calf, but he was working hard to achieve it.

What he got to eat were the ordinary calves from the pen. He could eat one daily if he pleased, but he couldn't touch the designated calf without the father's permission.

He lived with the hope that one day he could eat from that calf. One day he would earn the right for the calf to be killed to celebrate something the elder son had done.

This is what was happening with the tabernacle. Calves were sacrificed every day to alleviate people's guilt and to appease God. Every time someone did something they shouldn't have, a calf had to die.

But these were just shadows pointing to the predestined calf that had been prepared since before the foundation of the world, waiting for someone to do something that would require its death.

The fact that God required a sacrifice for guilt or sin was no accident; He wanted to show us the consequences of our actions.

From the first act of disobedience to God, in the Garden of Eden, when Adam and Eve had to leave that place, an animal had to die for them, and from that animal, the skin would be used to make garments for them.

They tried to cover their shame with fig leaves, easily going to a fig tree and cutting leaves to make aprons. Still, God wanted to teach them that great lesson:

sacrifice is required, the death of something to cover that shame.

The prodigal son did something that deserved the death of the predestined calf:

he wanted to return home, he wanted to go back to the father.

And the father deemed it appropriate that the calf, which had been predestined for a special occasion, found its purpose: to reconcile the father and his lost son.

The son didn't have to do anything extra to get the father to grant him that privilege. Even when the elder son confronted the father about why he gave the predestined calf to his brother, the father told him that everything he owns is also the elder son's. In other words, you could also have enjoyed the inheritance without having to leave home.

Now, as we stand in front of the bronze altar, we understand that we no longer have to bring any animal to be sacrificed for our guilt because the ultimate sacrifice has already been made.

The calf that had been predestined since before the foundation of the world achieved its purpose, which is to reconcile us with God, to reunite us with the father once more.

We have tried to do things our way, and it seems it hasn't worked.

We went far from home, thinking we could live without the father, creating our own version of the estate, only to end up with nothing.

No matter how much we want to work in the fields all day to earn the father's favor, it's impossible.

He was pleased to give us the predestined calf to celebrate our reconciliation.

To earn it, we've had to do nothing more than enter the tabernacle, pass through that curtain, stand in front of the altar, and admire the fact that God set the ransom for our rescue, and at the same time, He paid the price.

If that's His way of mending things between Him and me, then I have no choice but to surrender and let Him do things His way.

Chapter 22
New Attire

> *"But the father said to his servants, 'Bring out the best robe and put it on him;'"*
> (Luke 15:22)

> *"That you put off, concerning your former conduct, the old man which grows corrupt according to the deceitful lusts, and be renewed in the spirit of your mind, and that you put on the new man which was created according to God, in true righteousness and holiness."*
> (Ephesians 4:22-24)

Before continuing further into the tabernacle, I can't leave the altar without asking myself: if I had to leave something at the altar as a sacrifice, what would I leave?

Looking at the altar, it makes me think of all the people who, at one time or another, arrived there with an animal in tow. Fully aware that the animal wasn't to blame for what they had done themselves. But they were also conscious of the fact that the wages of sin is death, so it was essentially either their life or the animal's.

Before offering the sacrifice, they had to identify with the animal by placing a hand on its head. Symbolically, this act transferred the guilt from one to the other.

This makes me reflect on the idea that if God, during the moment of sacrifice, looked down, instead of seeing the guilty person, He would see the sacrifice. It's as if this animal covered the person by taking their place.

> *Blessed is the one whose transgressions are*
> *forgiven, whose sins are covered.*
> (Psalms 32:1)

Wait a minute! Isn't this exactly what God did in the Garden of Eden?

When Adam and Eve sinned, He used animal skins to cover them, to hide their nakedness.

> *And the Lord God made garments of skin for*
> *Adam and his wife and clothed them.*
> (Genesis 3:21)

Though these skins wouldn't last forever; the moment they wore out or got damaged, they would need to sacrifice another animal to make new garments to cover themselves.

It's the same thing that happened in the tabernacle - continual sacrifices to keep covering the guilt.

This leads me to the answer to the question I asked at the beginning of this chapter: if I had to leave something at the altar before continuing further into the tabernacle, it would be this animal skin robe that has been covering me from guilt and shame.

That debt has been paid. I believe we don't need it anymore.

By doing so, we would be allowing God to see us as we truly are. It would mean stripping ourselves naked before Him and showing our spirit. It would mean no longer hiding but reconnecting with Him.

And after millennia, answering the question that Adam avoided in the garden when God asked, "Where are you?"

Guilt and shame made Adam disconnect and try to hide from God.

The last thing Adam and Eve did before leaving the Garden of Eden was to cover themselves with animal skins. The first thing we do upon entering the tabernacle is to remove those skins, leaving them at the altar before continuing on our journey. A few steps ahead is the bronze basin.

It was a tub filled with water for a ritual of the priests; once they had offered their sacrifices, they would come to this basin to wash their hands and feet. After cleansing themselves, they were ready to enter the tabernacle.

This basin was made from the mirrors of the women from the village. They donated their mirrors to be melted down and shaped into this basin (Exodus 38:8). Since the basin was made from mirrors, I imagine it possessed the property of reflecting the images of the priests, allowing them to see themselves and ensure they had washed off every stain before entering the tabernacle.

We see the prodigal son return. After having spent time in a pigsty, he carried the smell and filth of that place. The father didn't mind embracing and kissing him in such a state, but he couldn't continue in those conditions.

The next step for him was to wash and don clean clothes. The new garments, as described in the parable of the prodigal son, are referred to as the best attire or the finest robe. Something that set him apart, something that made it easy to identify him as the son, as someone special.

As the son washed his face, he saw a mirror and, after a while, he could see the image of his father reflected in it. He could see his true identity, recognizing himself once more. He also had to discard the garments he wore during his stay at the other estate. He had to rid himself of everything that reminded him of what had transpired there.

He didn't need to remember it anymore. He had to close that chapter in his life.

I picture the prodigal son washing himself, staring intently into a mirror.

Returning to the priests, there was also a special garment for them. When God was speaking to Moses on the mountain, He gave specific instructions regarding the garments of the priests: type of fabric, colors, materials, shapes, quantities—everything was meticulously detailed.

Once they stood before the basin to wash themselves, they could see their reflection in it and rid themselves of any stain or impurity they might notice.

The garment they wore identified them as priests, as mediators between God and man. Their role was to bridge the gap, reconciling God with humanity.

When we arrive at the bronze basin, it's there that we find a purpose for our lives. It can't be that we only exist to one day approach the altar and offer a sacrifice for our sins, only to depart and return five minutes later to offer another for some new misdeed we've thought to commit. Once we leave behind the animal skin we've been sacrificing to renew our clothes and lay bare before God, it's time to take on the new garment. Upon wearing it, we discover our purpose: to represent God on earth, to mediate between God and humanity.

On one occasion, one of Jesus' disciples asked him to show them the Father. Jesus' response was that if they had seen Him, they had seen the Father.

That was Jesus' mission—to represent God on earth, to make God known through His life.

He is the High Priest. His purpose is to represent God to humanity.

The same happens to us at the bronze basin. Once we wash ourselves and put on the new garment, it's as if we clothe ourselves with Jesus, like priests. So that when the Father looks at us, He sees Jesus, and when the world looks at us, they see Jesus.

> *"Do not lie to each other, since you have taken off your old self with its practices and have put on the new self, which is being renewed in knowledge in the image of its Creator."*
> (Colossians 3:9-10)

Once we understand this, we can see our reflection in the bronze basin and see the image of God, see God's purpose, and see our purpose on Earth.

Up to this point, having visited the outer courtyard of the tabernacle, having been to the bronze altar and understood that Jesus, by taking our place as the sacrifice and giving His life for ours...

And having visited the bronze basin and put on the new garment so that God can see His son through us, the Father can say:

> *"For this son of mine was dead and is alive again; he was lost and is found..."*
> (Luke 15:24)

This is the work of Jesus within us, when the wages of sin is death, and it's a path where, regrettably, that's the end. Jesus comes and pays the price for us, and by doing so, He restores the life we had already lost.

We were dead, and now we live.

Once He has returned that life to us through His sacrifice, He places us back in the scene, in front of God. After being disconnected from Him, we are now clothed in His son.

So that when He looks at us, He sees Jesus.

Jesus took our garments, which represented the guilt and shame of not being able to stand before God, and took them to the cross.

And He gave us His robes of righteousness so that God would see us as free from guilt.

The purpose of Jesus' work is to make us children once more.

But now, as children, we have an inheritance for ourselves.

An inheritance that we can claim... today.

> *"And if the Spirit of Him who raised Jesus from the dead is living in you, He who raised Christ from the dead will also give life to your mortal bodies because of His Spirit who lives in you."*
> (Romans 8:11)

But to understand what we are being told, let's continue our journey to the Holy Place...

Chapter 23
The Feast

> *"But we had to celebrate and rejoice, for this brother of yours was dead and has begun to live, and was lost and has been found."*
> (Luke 15:32)

> *"Neither do people light a lamp and put it under a bowl. Instead, they put it on its stand, and it gives light to everyone in the house. In the same way, let your light shine before others, that they may see your good deeds and glorify your Father in heaven."*
> (Matthew 5:15-16)

In the tent of meeting, there was the bronze altar where sacrifices were presented to cover guilt and, in a way, be reconciled with God. Although humanity, from the beginning of history, has tried to justify itself or try to approach God by its own merits or try to mend that broken relationship, there has been no way to do so.

God Himself had to justify us through Jesus. He set the price that had to be paid, and He Himself paid it. When Adam and Eve disobeyed and were exposed, they felt ashamed to look at each other. Their first reaction was to try to fix the problem themselves, making aprons of fig leaves. Self-justification.

> *Therefore, since we have been justified through faith, we have peace with God through our Lord Jesus Christ."*
> (Romans 5:1)

In that same tent of meeting, further on, is the bronze basin, whose purpose was for the priests to wash after offering sacrifices and before entering the Holy Place. In this basin, they could see their reflection and correct whatever was needed. By then, they should already have their garments that distinguished them as priests.

This is the concept of regeneration. Jesus took our place on the altar so that we might take His place as priests, as sons.

> *"We clothe ourselves with Him so that when God looks at us, He sees Him in us."*
> (Romans 13:14).

After the basin, there's another curtain, which is the entrance to the Holy Place. Inside there are three more pieces of furniture. In this place, only the priests enter to perform tasks that no one else can see; no one else can witness what happens inside the Holy Place. That remains between the priests and God.

But when entering that place, everything we see there reminds us that we have a purpose. It's not just about being saved or justified and escaping the consequences of our actions. We were rescued with a purpose. We were separated from what we once were or from the old self, for new roles that have nothing to do with what we did before.

The concept of being set apart for a new purpose or for new activities is known in the Bible as sanctification or making holy.

Welcome to the Holy Place.

Upon opening the curtain and entering, the first thing that catches my eye is a candelabrum on my left side. It's a gold candelabrum, with seven branches that have flames at their tips, illuminating the tabernacle.

The priests had the duty of keeping this lamp lit all the time. It used pure olive oil as fuel.

Jesus mentioned that we are the light of the world, that a light is not lit to be placed under a pillow, but the purpose of this light is to shine for others. In doing so, we are displayed before the world, before others.

Once we choose to be priests or mediators between God and men, it is not an option for us to hide or try to be secret agents for God. The way God wants to manifest Himself to the world is through us. Jesus Himself said that when our light shone before men, they would glorify God.

The same happened with the prodigal son. Once he returned home, after cleansing himself from where he had come from, and was given a new robe, a great feast was made with all the people of the estate and those around.

> *When the elder brother questioned the father about the feast, the father told him that the reason for the feast was to show his son to others, to display him, to present him to others as his son who had been found*
> (Luke 15:32).

To place him in front of everyone, so that they would see him once more as the son, regardless of what he had done. By doing this, I imagine the son would even reconsider the thought of doing what he did again.

For a task like this, which is to represent God in front of others, God does not let us do it on our own. Even when Jesus resurrected and had to ascend to the Father again, he left this task to his disciples.

But with the task, He also left them the promise that they wouldn't have to do it alone, but they received help from the Holy Spirit. Jesus would breathe the Holy Spirit into them just as God breathed into Adam so that he became in His image.

> *"But you will receive power when the Holy Spirit comes on you; and you will be my witnesses in Jerusalem, and in all Judea and Samaria, and to the ends of the earth."*
> (Acts 1:8)

Once you decide to enter the holy place, you know that these tasks or missions that are given to you, you don't have to do them alone. God is providing the means for us to achieve it, giving us His Spirit so that we become in His image and can represent Him on earth.

> *"But the Advocate, the Holy Spirit, whom the Father will send in my name, will teach you all things and will remind you of everything I have said to you. The world cannot accept him, because it neither sees him nor knows him. But you know him, for he lives with you and will be in you."*
> (John 14:17)

Chapter 24
The Ring

"...and put a ring on his finger..."
(Luke 15:22)

For the flesh desires what is contrary to the Spirit, and the Spirit what is contrary to the flesh. They are in conflict with each other, so that you do not do whatever you want.
(Galatians 5:17)

Standing inside the curtain that gives access to the Holy Place, I now turn to my right and see a table. It is made of acacia wood and covered in gold.

The table measures about 92 centimeters in length, 46 centimeters in width, and 69 centimeters in height.

On this table are twelve unleavened loaves. Each week, the priests had to bake twelve loaves, with each loaf representing one of the twelve tribes of Israel.

They had to place these loaves on the table and leave them there for a week.

After the week, the following Sabbath, they had to gather and eat that bread.

Once you enter the Holy Place, you see food on a table. That food was not for God to eat. It was for the priests; it was a kind of ceremony they had to perform every Sabbath.

Food.

In the parable of the prodigal son, food is mentioned several times. It's said that when the prodigal son was away from home, there was a shortage, a famine in that region. This was what pushed the younger son to seek employment, assistance, and food.

Once you have crossed into the Holy Place, there's something you must bear in mind: you are a spirit within a body. Just as your body needs nourishment, so too does your spirit require sustenance to remain strong.

Our spirit is what connects us to God or the spiritual world.

> *"God is spirit, and his worshipers must worship in the Spirit and in truth."*
> (John 4:24)

> *"And without faith it is impossible to please God, because anyone who comes to him must believe that he exists and that he rewards those who earnestly seek him."*
> (Hebrews 11:6)

The prodigal son, when distant from the father, needed to feed his body. The sustenance he received was heavily dependent on where he was. When he was with the father, he ate at his table as family, partaking of the best the household had to offer. However, when he was away from the father, he ate whatever was given to him on the other estate. If he wasn't satisfied with what was provided, he longed to eat the food intended for the animals he tended.

Our bodies are guided by instincts that simply seek gratification, regardless of the means. Hunger. Thirst. Sexual. Survival, which means: rest when you need it, sleep, seek warmth when you're cold, cool down when you're hot.

Instincts will seek satisfaction by any means necessary. But they must be nourished; otherwise, they spiral out of control, as seen in the parable where the son desired to eat from the pig trough. There is a need for something or someone to oversee them.

When the prodigal son decided to return to his father, his elder brother attempted to feed his soul with reproaches, reminding him of his actions when he was away from the father. Even as the younger son was trying to better himself, showcasing it through improved decisions, the elder brother felt the need to remind him of his past.

Our soul, too, needs nourishment. Thoughts, feelings, emotions – they all need balance, equilibrium. Here, we have the younger brother trying to become better, striving to change his circumstances, but his mind is still filled with doubts about what is to come.

The foundation of the mind or soul is reality – what you can touch, see, hear, taste, and smell. And the prodigal son is on the brink of confronting this reality. The scenes he played out in his head the previous night were merely figments of his imagination. There is no concrete evidence that everything will unfold as he envisioned, which might be causing some anxiety within him.

The elder brother would ensure to make this reality more burdensome, feeding his mind with memories of past mistakes, attacking his conscience. Making him believe that he doesn't deserve this reality, that he should be facing the consequences of his actions.

He shouldn't be receiving grace.

Because the mind doesn't understand grace; it cannot process it. It's not part of its reality. On one hand, we have the elder brother trying to rationalize the situation, reminding us that we do not deserve what's happening. This is mainly because he doesn't comprehend it himself.

On the other hand, there's the father, placing a ring on our finger—a ring signifying recognition as part of the family, as part of the spiritual realm. This is something we mustn't forget, a ring we cannot lose again—a symbol of belonging to him.

The instincts will continue to hunger, they will always seek satisfaction. The mind will persistently try to provide us with a reality based solely on its understanding. Our spirit needs nourishment to help maintain a balance in our daily lives.

When the prodigal son decided to return, among the options in his head, he never imagined he'd get another chance. His mind could not conceive that as a possibility. But the father had moved beyond that, and his sense of justice was far from conventional.

To grasp this, one must step into a new reality:

We are spirits entering the spiritual realm where God offers a fresh reality, wherein he calls us justified, where he identifies us as his children. In this realm, God presents us with a ring that recognizes us as heirs. This gesture transcends mere materialistic possession—it's a manifestation of God's endless love and grace, affirming our place in his eternal kingdom.

Recognizing us as part of His family.

And as we are children, we can't eat like the animals. As we are spirits, we must nourish them.

> *The Spirit itself bears witness with our spirit that we are children of God. And if children, then heirs—heirs of God and joint heirs with Christ, provided we suffer with Him in order that we may also be glorified with Him.*
> (Romans 8:16-17)

Chapter 25
Footwear

> *... And shoes on his feet.*
> (Luke 15:22)

> *For you did not receive the spirit of bondage again to fear, but you received the Spirit of adoption by whom we cry out, "Abba, Father!"*
> (Romans 8:15)

Now, standing at the door or curtain of the holy place, we look straight ahead, to the back of the space, and we can see another altar. This altar is the altar of incense.

It measured approximately 46 centimeters by 46 centimeters by almost one meter in height.

> *On this altar, incense was burned for certain rituals. When God was giving instructions to Moses about the tabernacle, He gave Moses the specific recipe to make this incense*
> (Exodus 30:34-38).

In fact, He ordered that no one try to copy this recipe for personal use, let alone attempt to offer a different type of incense than the one He specified.

The aroma of this incense helped to counteract the smell of the blood and the sacrifices that were presented in the tabernacle.

> *The day the high priest entered the most holy place, he had to be covered by a cloud of incense so as not to die.*
> (Leviticus 16:13)

> *And from the angel's hand, the smoke of the incense,*
> *with the prayers of the saints, ascended before God.*
> (Revelation 8:4)

Incense has symbolism in the Bible; it is used to compare it with prayers. It's as if, when we speak to God, those words rise up like a cloud towards Him, and He enjoys what He is witnessing at that moment.

But... what does incense have to do with the prodigal son's new shoes?

In the culture where the parable that Jesus is telling takes place, employees or slaves were the people who did not wear shoes; at times, being barefoot denoted poverty. When the prodigal son returned from that distant region where he had been working with pigs, he did so without shoes.

Now the father told his servants to give him shoes because his status had changed drastically. He arrives at his father's house, and his position is restored.

He was no longer a slave; he was a son.

And as we learned before, even if one wanted to be just a day laborer, doing only what is asked to receive a salary without any kind of relationship or commitment – we are sons and daughters. As part of the family, there is a relationship, and therefore communication.

That is what the incense in the tabernacle reminds us of; God enjoys communication with us. Every time we take the time to speak to Him, it's a moment God sees as incense, a pleasant fragrance before Him.

> *And because you are sons, God has sent forth the Spirit of*
> *His Son into your hearts, crying out, "Abba, Father!"*
> *So you are no longer a slave, but a son; and if a*
> *son, then an heir of God through Christ.*
> (Galatians 4:6-7)

Once shoes were placed on the prodigal son's feet, his status changed from a day laborer to a son. The people present would start seeing him differently; he had to begin seeing himself differently. His new position granted him a place in his father's house where he belonged.

Part of the family, and that included communication to get to know each other better, after the time he had been away, after all the experiences, after the changes that occurred on the estate, there was much to discuss.

Chapter 26
The Cherubim with a New Job
(Reflection)

The cherubim guarding the path to the tree of life when Adam and Eve were expelled from paradise. Entrusted to ensure that no one entered paradise, he was given a blazing sword in case someone decided to return. He was ready to fight; that was his job. Ready to defend the path to the tree. As long as he was present, no one would dare enter. Or so he thought.

Years passed, and there was no action. No one wanted to return. Humanity continued walking in the opposite direction. Further and further away.

During the day, he practiced new moves with his sword. Battle stances. Gestures to intimidate any who might approach. He paced back and forth, awaiting action. A mission was assigned to him, and he just wanted to fulfill it. He yearned to return to God and report on everything he had done that day. How many people tried to come back and eat from the tree, and how he stopped them. How many battles he fought daily to fulfill his mission. To show war marks on his armor. Scars from battles.

The only action he saw was in his imagination.

No one wanted to approach. He never got the chance.

He lost his job. He became unemployed.

Many years passed, and no one approached the tree.

There was no need for anyone to guard it anymore.

The cherubim might have done a great job.

There was a reason he was chosen. But he never got the chance.

One day, the cherubim saw a job advertisement:

Two cherubim needed.

Position title: Mercy Seat.

Duties: to be above the Ark of the Covenant, symbolizing the throne of God.

To be the place where God and man meet.

To be the place where God reveals Himself to communicate with humanity.

To be the place where man can come and taste the tree of life.

To bring man closer to God so he can have a taste, a glimpse of eternity.

That's the meaning of propitiate: to make something happen.

To bring the two terms closer so that they meet.

To be the place where two parties approach.

And come to an agreement.

To be the place where, at last, what seemed impossible, exists.

What was once an illusion is now real.

Where humanity finds the gateway to the spiritual world.

Creator and creation speaking again.

No need to bring a sword to the new job.

No intimidating faces required.

The cherubim's new role is to invite entry into paradise.

Now, every time someone approaches the tree of life, the cherubim must celebrate it.

They had to throw a party.

The cherubim's new job would be to organize a celebration for those who chose to return.

Jesus himself said it:

> *"I tell you, there is rejoicing in the presence of the angels of God over one sinner who repents."*
> (Luke 15:10)

Chapter 27
New Residence

> *"Let them construct a sanctuary for Me,*
> *that I may dwell among them."*
> (Exodus 25:8)

> *"You shall place the mercy seat on top of the ark, and in*
> *the ark you shall put the testimony which I will give to*
> *you. There I will meet with you; and from above the mercy*
> *seat, from between the two cherubim which are upon the*
> *ark of the testimony, I will speak to you about all that I*
> *will give you in commandment for the sons of Israel."*
> (Exodus 25:21-22)

When God gave Moses the instructions for the construction of the tabernacle, and once it was completed, God intended to use this tabernacle as His dwelling place. Whenever Moses wanted to consult with God, He would speak to him from the ark. When priests were consecrated for the maintenance of the tabernacle, they made sure that everything was in order and all established rites or ceremonies were performed.

However, there was one area of the tabernacle to which they had no access: the Most Holy Place, where the Ark of the Covenant was located. Entering this sacred space was so delicate that there's a story in the Book of Leviticus about two young men who entered to offer incense as an offering to God. Upon entering uninvited, fire burst forth from the ark, consuming them. They hadn't been instructed to perform this act, thus they had no permission to enter there.

On another occasion, when they were transporting the Ark of the Covenant from one place to another on a cart pulled by oxen, the oxen stumbled on the path. It seemed that the Ark would fall off the cart. In a rush of impulse, a man named Uzzah stretched out his hand to steady it. However, the moment he touched the Ark, he was struck down and died. This serves as a poignant reminder of the sacredness and the untouchable nature of the Ark.

These historical episodes underscore the gravitas that surrounded any attempt to access the divine uninvited. Even when done with good intentions, a strict protocol was in place, and any deviation from it could have fatal consequences.

Yet, in the religious calendar of the Israelites, there was a day specifically chosen by God for atonement – Yom Kippur, or the Day of Atonement. On this day, the high priest would enter the Holy of Holies to present a sacrifice to atone for the sins of the entire nation.

To be allowed this privilege, the high priest had to undergo rigorous preparation. He needed to be found worthy and had to avoid the tragic fates like those mentioned above. The purification rites for the high priest were extensive. He needed to be in a state of perfection: spiritually cleansed, having offered sacrifices for his own sins, and remaining blameless.

A notable part of his attire was a set of bells attached to the hem of his robe. These bells served a unique purpose: they were an auditory sign of his well-being. As he moved within the Holy of Holies, the bells would ring, signaling to those outside that he was still alive and moving. Given that he could enter the Holy of Holies just once a year, he had ample time to prepare for this sacred task.

Such was the seriousness, reverence, and preparation required for one to aspire to come into contact with God…

Imagine that the prodigal son, after all that happened in the distant province where he was, decides to return home. After a long and tiring journey under the sun, trying to find the right words to explain why the father should hire him back as an employee.

He arrives at where his father's estate used to be, only to realize it's no longer there; the father has moved, relocated his estate and all his possessions elsewhere.

Imagine the look on the prodigal son's face: surprise, confusion, uncertainty.

His gaze would reflect a thousand questions.

His new mission: to find the new address. To find his father at all costs.

I know it's hard to imagine this because it's not how the story goes, but it was a thought that crossed my mind for a moment: What if this had happened?

It didn't happen to the prodigal son, but it happened to us, to the rest of humanity.

When we decided to return to God and make peace with Him, we expected to find a God who would judge us for all we've done, a God who would assign us tasks to make up for our wrongs. A God whom we couldn't even look at for fear of death.

We expected to meet the God of the Ark of the Covenant.

We returned to Him in fear, in shame, expecting a reprimand.

But once we approached the Ark, we realized He wasn't in there anymore.

Now it's us with a thousand questions, the first one being: Where did He move to?

Let me give you the new address:

You flip the pages of your Bible until you enter the New Testament,...

You keep moving forward until you reach the letter to the Hebrews.

You enter there, and look for chapter 4.

You scroll slowly until you find verse number 14, there you stop.

And you read slowly until verse 16.

You've reached your destination.

I took the liberty of saving you the journey and brought it to you.

This is what you will find:

> "Seeing then that we have a great High Priest who has passed through the heavens, Jesus the Son of God, let us hold fast our confession. For we do not have a High Priest who cannot sympathize with our weaknesses, but was in all points tempted as we are, yet without sin. Let us therefore come boldly to the THRONE OF GRACE, that we may obtain mercy and find grace to help in time of need."
> (Hebrews 4:14-16)

If you want to find God, the place where you'll do so is at the throne of grace.

A place where there's no judgment, no rebukes, you won't die for daring to approach Him.

On the contrary, you'll find a purpose to live for.

A place where the High Priest intercedes for you because he understands you, because he went through the same.

Because he lived in a flesh body like ours.

And unlike the Ark of the Covenant, where only the high priest had access once a year, to the throne of grace you have access 364 days of the year.

But... why 364 days? What about the other day?

What? Doesn't a year have 365 days?

Well, unlike the Ark of the Covenant, the only day you don't have access to the throne of grace is that day you feel perfect.

That day you believe you deserve to be there on your own merits.

That day you think you are self-sufficient.

That day you believe you've done enough to enter that place.

That day you believe you can impress God.

That's the only day of the year you don't have access to the throne, because it seems you don't need His grace.

The days you feel you don't deserve His attention,

The days you lost count of the times you've fallen and gotten up again,

The days you can't stand to look in the mirror because your own reflection judges you,

The days you have nowhere to go or no one to go with…

You are more than welcome at the throne of grace.

Now it's easier to imagine if this had happened to the prodigal son in the story.

But thank God it happened to us.

Chapter 28
Dressed for the Occasion

> *"He shall put on the holy linen tunic, and the linen undergarments shall be next to his body; he shall be girded with the linen sash and attired with the linen turban. These are holy garments; he shall bathe his body in water and then put them on."*
> (Leviticus 16:4)

> *"And when they go into the inner court to minister in the sanctuary, they shall put on linen garments; they shall have nothing of wool on them while they minister at the gates of the inner court or within it. They shall have linen turbans on their heads and linen undergarments on their bodies. They shall not bind themselves with anything that causes sweat."*
> (Ezekiel 44:17-18)

As I mentioned earlier, while they were in the desert journeying to the Promised Land, God had given them specific instructions to build a tabernacle where He would dwell. Every aspect was meticulously detailed: shapes, colors, dimensions...

When it came to the attire of the priests, God had a clear vision of how they should look. One detail that struck me was the fabric of the priests' garments: linen.

Considering they were living in the desert, it makes sense. They needed a fabric that would help them cope with the climate.

That's one of linen's properties: it helps you stay cool in the heat. This would certainly assist the priests who worked full-time in the tabernacle. God specifically mentioned He didn't want them wearing anything that could induce sweat.

What could possibly remind God of someone sweating while serving Him in the tabernacle? What might sweat represent in God's service?

To answer that, we'd have to go back to the very beginning, to the Garden of Eden. Recall the moment when Adam and Eve tasted the forbidden fruit, which changed their entire perspective. They felt shame and sewed fig leaves to cover their nakedness.

They had everything they needed in the garden. However, after their disobedience, their circumstances drastically changed. God had promised to provide for them, but now, having chosen their own path, they were cast out. They now had to earn their living, food, and shelter.

God told Adam that from now on, he would eat bread by the sweat of his brow (Genesis 3:17-19). He would have to toil and labor for his sustenance.

A day's work for a wage.

To do to achieve.

To sweat to accomplish something.

That was the last thing God wanted the priest to think, or even us, that we are earning our place in His presence.

That we achieve standing before Him by our merits.

That we earn a place or position by what we have done.

That we can stand before Him with our face covered in sweat and say: I did it!

When God was about to expel Adam and Eve from the garden, the book of Genesis mentions that God made them tunics of skins to cover their nakedness. An animal had to be sacrificed to take its skin and use it to make tunics for them. To cover them.

Once this fabric deteriorated, now they had to kill an animal to get the skin and make another tunic to continue covering them.

That was the same concept in the tabernacle with the sacrifices.

Animals were sacrificed on the altar to cover the guilt of the person offering it.

Animal sacrifices to cover.

Another detail in this passage from Ezekiel 44 is that when God was giving instructions about the priests' attire, verse 17 mentions that they cannot enter the tabernacle wearing any garment made of wool. (We know that woolen fabric comes from animals).

This fabric represents sacrifices to cover us.

> *Knowing that a man is not justified by the works of the law but by the faith in Jesus Christ, we have believed in Jesus Christ that we might be justified by faith in Christ and not by the works of the law; for by the works of the law no flesh shall be justified.*
> (Galatians 2:16)

God's request to leave behind any fabric made of animal before entering His presence is a nod to the fact that after the sacrifice Jesus made on the cross, there are no more sacrifices needed to cover or justify guilt.

There's absolutely nothing you can do to earn your place before God.

There's no price you can pay to be justified in the eyes of God.

There's nothing we can do to impress God.

For on the day you think you can impress Him, remember, it's the only day you can't access Him.

Although, reading about Jesus's life in the gospels, I stumbled upon passages where people did impress Him. Want to know what impresses Him?

> "When Jesus heard it, He marveled, and said to those who followed, 'Assuredly, I say to you, I have not found such great faith, not even in Israel.'"
> (Matthew 8:10)

Why is having faith so impressive to Him?

Because in the world we live in, everything is earned through labor. We must act to get what we desire. We are used to getting what we deserve and taking credit for having achieved it.

Even the prodigal son, upon returning to the father, wanted to earn his acceptance, he wanted to be hired, he wanted to earn his shelter and food through work.

In his mind he believed, he was convinced that he did not deserve them.

The word grace is not used often.

And for someone to come and tell you that they accept you and take you back without you having to do anything in return, it seems impossible to us.

And for the one telling you this to be God himself.

It's hard to believe.

Even more so when we are at the lowest point in our life.

Have faith?

Believe in something I can't see yet? (that's the definition of faith)

Do I just have to trust him?

No more sacrifices, no more rituals, no more ostentatious garments, no more sweat... just faith.

Believe that he is enough.
Believe that he paid the price for you.
Believe that he tore the veil to give us access to God.
Believe that he clothes you with his own garments of righteousness.

Believe that he has washed you with his own blood.
This is what the prodigal son did, he
believed what his father told him.
He accepted the robe, the ring, the shoes.
He accepted what came with that.
He accepted the new covenant.
He accepted the inheritance.
He accepted being a son.

Chapter 29
God in a Box
(Reflection)

I was walking in my office listening to music.
Suddenly, I found myself standing in front of a bookshelf.
On one of my shelves, there is a special cube.
Reserved for just one item.
This cube is covered with a red curtain.
This curtain is torn in the middle.
The point of this cube is just that; you can
open the curtain and look inside.
Inside, there's a replica of the Ark of the Covenant.
I can take it in my hands.
I can lift its lid and peer inside.
I can admire the details on it.
This time I took it in my hands and asked myself a question:
What if the story had been different?
What if the curtain had never been torn?
Where would we be if God was still inside a box?
If only a perfect person had access to him once a year.
And we lived in the Old Testament times.
And God was inside a box.
Where access to him was through ceremonies and rituals.
Through sacrifices.
And we had to be literally perfect in order
to access him, once a year.
Many of us want to see God as the God of the Old Testament.
We want to keep him inside that box.

The prodigal son felt the same way when
he thought about returning.
He believed that the father wouldn't take him back as a son.
But we've already seen that story throughout the book.
It's time to tell our story.
What happened after the welcome party?
How was the relationship with the father?

I was supposed to write one more chapter.
That was the plan, my plan.
A chapter that contrasted the Old and New Testaments.
But I realized that the information I was going to write in
this chapter had already been written by someone else.
Whoever wrote the letter to the Hebrews, especially chapter 9.
Read this:

So, for that reason, he is the mediator of a new covenant, so
that death having taken place for the redemption of the
transgressions committed under the first covenant, those who
are called may receive the promise of an eternal inheritance.
For where there is a testament, the death of the
one who made it must be confirmed.
For a testament is valid only when people are dead, since
it is never in force while the one who made it is alive.
For Christ did not enter a sanctuary made with human
hands that was only a copy of the true one; he entered
heaven itself, now to appear for us in God's presence;
And not to offer himself again and again, as the high priest enters
the Most Holy Place every year with blood that is not his own.
Otherwise, he would have had to suffer again and
again since the foundation of the world.
But as it is, he has appeared once for all at the culmination
of the ages to do away with sin by the sacrifice of himself.
(Hebrews 9:15-17, 24-26)

The moment Jesus dies, the curtain is torn. And the Ark is exposed
for all to see. At that moment, humanity has access to him.

The moment the testator dies, a new covenant is made.
A new testament. Where the tabernacle is the person
himself. And God Himself lives within us.

I will put my laws in their hearts, And I will write
them on their minds. (Hebrews 10:16)

Now we become the box where God makes His dwelling.
Instead of the tablets of the commandments that were inside the
Ark, These laws are inscribed on our hearts to live for Him.
He will convey to us the laws so that we live as He desires.
He does this through the Holy Spirit, who communicates
to us what God wants from us.
Now we are tabernacles that God will use to manifest Himself.
That is the new covenant.
That is the New Testament.
That is the new inheritance.
It depends on us, If we want to put Him back inside a box.

Chapter 30
The Second Eve

And so it is written: The first man Adam became a living being; the last Adam, a life-giving spirit. The first man was of the dust of the earth; the second man is the Lord from heaven.
(1 Corinthians 15:45,47)

Let us rejoice and be glad and give him glory! For the wedding of the Lamb has come, and his bride has made herself ready. Fine linen, bright and clean, was given her to wear. (Fine linen stands for the righteous acts of the holy people.)
(Revelation 19:7-8)

This book began with the story of creation and paradise, and I wanted to finish it in the same place. But first, there are pieces that I need to move to show the complete scene.

Adam's Purpose:

When God created Adam, He had a plan for him, He made him with a purpose: the first chapter of Genesis shows us God's mind when He envisioned Adam. He wanted to make him in His image; He wanted him to be an extension of Himself, to represent Him, so that when someone looked at Adam, they would see God through him.

Furthermore, another purpose for Adam was to rule over creation.

To govern the animals and the earth. In a way, to have control over everything, to be the steward of creation.

But man didn't just want to be a steward; he wanted to be a god.

He wanted full control, not having to answer to anyone.

To do as he pleased, without having to explain himself.

So Adam took his own path.

The Purpose of the Second Adam:

God could not let humanity drift away. Even though He had given them free will, He had to find a way to draw them back to Him.

So God sent His Son. Someone who would fulfill the purpose of the first Adam. Someone who could represent Him, be His image.

Jesus lived up to God's expectations.

He knew how to represent Him.

He even said that whoever has seen Him has seen the Father.

He took control over nature, calming storms, multiplying food, healing sick bodies, even having control over death itself.

That was precisely God's plan for humanity, for others to see God through us.

So that when someone doubted the existence of God, they only had to look at His representatives.

That's what Jesus came to do on earth.

To show us how it's done.

The Purpose of Eve:

God saw that Adam was alone. Even though he was surrounded by creation, and he kept busy naming the animals, and organizing or managing, even learning from what he was seeing, since everything was new to him.

He had no one to talk to, no one to share his experience with, he had no partner. He saw that the animals had someone else of their kind.

But he was unique.

So God decided to give him help, to give him someone like him. And he made him fall into a deep sleep, and while Adam slept, God opened his side, and from there he brought out Eve.

Someone with whom he could share all his experiences and who would understand what he was talking about. Someone who would speak his same language.

Someone who would complete him.

The Purpose of the Second Eve:

When Jesus was on earth, his words were not understood by anyone.

What he tried to teach was not accepted.

His doctrine did not fit with the people around him.

They didn't understand what he was trying to do.

Although he could control nature, one area he couldn't touch without permission was free will.

So people did not accept him and decided to get rid of him.

He was alone in a world that preferred to ignore the spiritual realm.

He was alone in a world that wanted to follow the law he was trying to reform.

He was alone in his mission to bring humanity back to being the image of God again.

So God decides to give him a suitable help.

To give him someone who would understand what he was talking about.

Someone who wanted to help with that mission.

The Birth of the Second Eve:

Jesus is on the cross. Alone once more. He knows the plan.

Everything were shadows pointing to this moment. Nothing is a surprise to him.

So he decides to enter into a deep sleep (from which he knows he will awake in three days).

And as he sleeps… his side is opened.

One of the soldiers pierces his side, and what came out was blood and water (John 19:34).

At that moment, a new way to the holy of holies is opened.

> *By a new and living way opened for us*
> *through the curtain, that is, his body.*
> (Hebrews 10:20)

No more sacrifices are required after that moment, Jesus was making the final sacrifice. And the only entrance that existed to the holy of holies, where the ark of the covenant was, where one person, once a year, could enter into the presence of God, is nullified.

There is now a new way, a new entrance where everyone has access through Jesus.

And the key to that door is faith.

> *Let us draw near to God with a sincere heart and*
> *with the full assurance that faith brings, having our*
> *hearts sprinkled to cleanse us from a guilty conscience*
> *and having our bodies washed with pure water.*
> (Hebrews 10:22)

Blood and Water

When we looked at the section of the Tabernacle or the path back to the Father, Jesus' work is described in the outer part of the Tabernacle: the altar of sacrifices, and the bronze basin.

The blood of Jesus paved the way to pay for our sins, to atone for our guilt. His blood is what covers us so that we can enter into God's presence. So that when God looks upon us, He sees the blood, and we are justified before Him.

Water is what cleanses us and keeps us clean. It regenerates us. It's not enough to be justified and have access to God. As mentioned earlier, the purpose of the second Eve is to be a suitable helper for the second Adam. And that's where this group of people who understand God's purpose for the world and speak the language of the second Adam comes into the scene. That is where the church is born.

Water is what regenerates us and cleanses us from everything that reminded us of who we once were. It cleanses our conscience so that we can dedicate ourselves to fulfilling our purpose.

This purpose is found when entering the Holy Place, and we find the work of the Holy Spirit, something we also saw when studying the lampstand, the table of the bread of presence, and the altar of incense.

Blood and water are what pave our way into God's presence.

> *After this, I looked, and behold, a great multitude, which no one could number, from every nation, tribe, people, and language, standing before the throne and before the Lamb, clothed in white robes, with palm branches in their hands. Then one of the elders addressed me, saying: "Who are these, clothed in white robes, and from where have they come?" I said to him, "Sir, you know." And he said to me, "These are the ones who have come out of the great tribulation; they have washed their robes and made them white in the blood of the Lamb."*
> (Revelation 7:9,13-14)

The prodigal son couldn't wear the new garments without first washing himself with water. Similarly, the priests couldn't wear their garments without washing first. The same is true for the church. Another passage in Revelation, which I used to open this chapter, refers to the church as the bride of the Lamb.

The wife of the second Adam:

> *"And it was granted her to clothe herself with fine linen, bright and pure"*— *for the fine linen is the righteous deeds of the saints.*
> (Revelation 19:8)

We know that actions or deeds don't open the door to heaven for us. When the Bible refers to deeds, it uses the Greek word "ergon," meaning work, effort, or action. However, when it speaks of "righteous deeds," it uses a single word: "Dikaiomatos." More than just actions, this refers to a mindset where what you do is genuine, where you don't have to strain to behave in a particular way. It's where what emerges from you is righteousness. You don't have to contemplate how you should act. These are the garments one acquires once they are cleansed.

This is what I mean by being a suitable helper for the second Adam.

Paradise:

When Adam and Eve were in paradise, in some ways, Eve took control of the situation when she ate from the tree of knowledge and gave some to Adam to follow in her footsteps. Eve took control, and both were expelled from paradise.

This time, it's different. This time, it's the second Adam who takes control, becoming the head and guide of the two, fulfilling the purpose or mission given to them. When the second Adam takes control, the animal skin garments turn into fine linen. When the second Adam takes control, he brings us back to the paradise from which we were once expelled.

When the second Adam takes control, we understand that the missing link connecting us to a supreme being is within us. Our spirit, which has been hidden all this time beneath this flesh, beneath emotions, beneath pretenses, beneath filters. But one day, just as to leave paradise Adam and Eve were covered with skins, to return to paradise we will have to leave that body behind.

> *"When the perishable has been clothed with the imperishable, and the mortal with immortality, then the saying that is written will come true: Death has been swallowed up in victory."*
> (1 Corinthians 15:54)

When the second Adam takes control...

One day he will take the hand of the second Eve,
And together they will walk back to paradise,
He will lead her back to the tree of life,
And he will cut a fruit from the tree,
And he will give it to her to eat...
And they will live happily EVER AFTER.

www.ingramcontent.com/pod-product-compliance
Lightning Source LLC
LaVergne TN
LVHW091551060526
838200LV00036B/789